MANAGING CHANGE IN THE CHURCH

Douglas W. Johnson

FRIENDSHIP PRESS • NEW YORK

dedicated to my
departed teachers
in local churches

Walter
Leslie

Library of Congress Cataloging in Publication Data

Johnson, Douglas W   1934-
  Managing change in the church.
  Includes bibliographical refer-
  ences.
   1. Church renewal.   I. Title.
BV600.2.J56   254   74-12458
ISBN 0-377-00017-5

contents

1. Affirmations 5

2. Pluralism 10

3. World Views 19

4. Owners and Participants 30

5. Decisions 45

6. Conflict 54

7. Practicalism and Theology 67

8. Change and Organizations 79

9. A New Mystery 90

Notes 96

preface

This book is my affirmation of the strength and vitality of the church. Wherever I go, people are struggling to make their church an institution responsive to human need, attentive to divine call and actively leading toward a disciplined and dedicated life. These are not easily reachable goals; frustration is often the lot of these people. Yet, as they strive, they learn. As they share their learnings, they develop a fellowship with others who are also learning. It is the purpose of this book to share learnings so that the fellowship of strivers can be extended.

The learnings stand as examples and we are called upon to adapt them for our use. They can inspire or they can defeat. It is up to us to let them lead during these times of change. In this spirit of challenge, the insights here can encourage even those who might be ready to give up.

No one travels a road alone. In my traveling there have been patient and wonderfully kind people who have provided much of the basis for this effort. It may be that I have missed in some detail their hopes and expectations for the church and for us who compose it. I think, however, the thrust of their lives and faith are contained in the examples and theology that underlie this book.

This is a work book. It is designed to be used more than once. It is an effort to help us untangle ourselves and get to the task of the church.

1 affirmations

Change is activity. It does not have to be, indeed should not be, a frantic search for just any activity but, in a Christian context, is a way of doing things to make a difference to oneself and others. Change is activity with its purpose rooted in the message and manner of Christ.

This book deals with various types of change we all experience. The suggestions for dealing with change and resistance to it come from my own experience and that of others. Suggestions for coping with change are proposed here because they have worked in actual situations. They are also based upon a particular understanding of the gospel of love, which should temper all efforts to deal with change for a Christian.

Each of us approaches any subject or issue with several assumptions. So that we are clear during the remainder of the book, let us look at some of the assumptions that undergird the chapters that follow.

1. Change requires us to do and act. Jesus said, Go and do. (Matthew 10) However, our inclination is not toward action but more nearly to talking about doing something. For example, we can all see ourselves in the following scene.

"You know, Joe, we ought to go by and see Lee. She isn't feeling well and it might do her good to have a visit."

"I know, Helen, but I just don't feel like it."

"You never feel like it. We ought to go."

"Well, you go. I don't feel like it!"

"Forget it!"

We are like these people, too often. We know what we ought to do but somehow cannot take the first step. We "ought" our way through life—until we are caught either by an inspiration or by the absolute necessity of getting something accomplished. Then we start moving and find that deadlines are met, problems are confronted and things are done. Often, after a task is finished, we are glad to have been a part of it. In fact, "we wouldn't have missed it for anything!"

In the church it is much easier to deal in the *ought's* and *probably's* than it is to make decisions and take action. It is easier because in talking *about* a decision we can always say "if." We can make our own action conditional on someone else's. For example, "If she says that one more time I'm going to have to set her straight." Or, "If that racist lets go with his propaganda once more, I'm going to tell him off." Or, "If they would only ask me, I would get active in their club."

As Christians many of us feel better for having thought or said what we would do "if." We know that talking makes little difference; yet it is our way of getting off the hook. We know the conditions of discipleship (for example, Matthew 25) but are unwilling to pay the price. In our efforts to have the best of both worlds, we make Christianity conditional—on our own needs.

We need to stop sitting around thinking about what we ought to do and get down to business. We need to speak out for justice! We need to show love and toleration! We need to give to others! We need to listen to God and people! We need to do and be rather than retreat, excuse or hope vain hopes. We need to dream of the promise of God through Christ and then do our utmost to make the dream a reality.

2. We are accountable to God and to other people for our action and inaction.

An action demands an explanation . . . a reason . . . a because, especially when change or innovation results. Paul was identified as one of a group who were turning the world upside down. (Acts 17:6-9) His "because" came from an episode on the road to Damascus. (Acts 9:1-22) While we may not have such a dramatic event on which to base our actions, the reasons for our acting must be founded on a life experience as real as Paul's.

3. Related to this solid basis for personal action must be a conscious recognition of our place in the stream of God's creation. History does not start and end with us. We are a part of an ongoing experience of human kind. It behooves us to recognize that our efforts at change involve other people and their histories.

We should not tamper with either people or history without a very good reason, and even then with a great deal of humility. The reason for tampering, from the point of view of a Christian, comes from a commitment to Christ and the inspiration of the Holy Spirit, and also an intelligent reading of history and trends.

4. Change occurs at a particular time in history, that is, it is always a link in the human historical process. A Christian strategy of change protects this sense of continuity with the

past, the present and the future. While a change may seem to be sudden, it is built upon accumulated pieces of human experiences. These come from the past and are used in the present so that situations, conditions or events will be different in the future.

5. People need a sense of continuity. A person cannot separate personhood from either past events or present activities. These are a part of each person just as are her or his eyes, ears and nose. Once a person does something or is something, that can never be separated from him or her. Neither can an individual look to the future without taking into account the wholeness of what has been incorporated into his or her life by previous experience.

A person is the needle bringing the thread of humanness through the warp and woof of others to make a total fabric of life. Christ, as a reference and inspiration point, brings the wholeness of the church to bear upon human situations. The Christian thus has both humanness and divine experiences, which enrich this fabric called life. Each person is a part of the train of saints and sinners working together through Christ to make this world into a dream.

6. The Christian dealing with change protects the personhood and wholeness of individuals affected by the change. This is possible only when personhood is seen as a gift of God's presence now, while recognizing that the present is shaped by the past and the future is part of the hopes, expectations and purposes gained from both.

Even persons who have experienced religious salvation in a sudden, dramatic fashion bring with them a past which continues to influence and direct them in the future. That past and the future is always focused upon the person. Taking a cue from Christ, Paul gave the church a charge to look to each person as important and essential to God's kingdom. It is a precious heritage of the church and one which should not be obscured by clamoring for efficiency, effectiveness and budget trimming.

7. Change should be focused. Jesus talked specifically about money and possessions to people who had problems with these. (Mark 10:24; Luke 6:24; Luke 12:20) He spoke to the people who were troubled about riches. He talked about their faith. He told them exactly what they should do. (Luke 18:22)

Change is useful only when it is focused and specific. To call for change in general is like being in favor of good health.

The idea is good but it has no focus. On the other hand, preventing tooth decay by brushing one's teeth three times a day is specific and focused. In fact, good health is achieved and maintained by making a series of specific changes in one's habits, not by speaking in generalities.

8. A Christian understands change as a continuous stream of specific issues. Personal change is really an endless train of small changes in attitudes and habits; change in an organization takes place as a series of small adjustments.

9. Until a change is assimilated into the habit and myth systems of people, it is not effective. Small specific changes provide people an opportunity to absorb and own new styles of acting at a relatively comfortable rate. They can also develop new myths about life more easily when change is segmented. Small specific changes also allow people to have a chance to develop new habits, which incorporate the changes.

10. A Christian views change as a pattern for the whole of life. A philosopher told us that when we consecutively throw two stones into a river or pond, we do not throw them into the same pond or river. The very presence of one additional stone changes the river or pond so that what was, is not now. He used this story to illustrate the process of life which changes each moment. Even though a person may feel as though he or she has been in that place and had that experience before, time, events and experiences forbid it.

Anyone who has gone "home" for a class reunion is struck with the amount of change in people. Age, illness and death keep us cycling through life. We are not and can never be what we were yesterday or the day before. It is imperative for the Christian, therefore, not to spend a great deal of time, effort or money trying to *regain* some past experience. It is more important to spend time and effort on developing an attitude and expectation for living in the present.

11. The Christian recognizes that other people are involved with us in initiating and dealing with change. We do not live as isolates. We are bound together with others just by being alive in the same place and at the same time.

12. As our ideas and experiences change, we create new situations. These provide us with opportunities to make new friends as well as new enemies. As we decide and act, we are living in new days that God gives us to live for him. Jesus did not say anything about the living being easy; rather, he said the opposite. (Matthew 10:34-42) He told us to live in total

dedication. In so doing, we will be new persons in new surroundings.

Christians engage in change with Jesus Christ as the inspiration. He is our strength and hope. His message is our basis for acting. The spontaneity and reality of our concern for our world neighbors become the boundaries of our selfishness.

As we walk, run or trudge through life, some of the techniques and practices described in following chapters will be helpful. The most important thing to remember, however, is that we are a part of God's continuously changing creation with all the hope and promise that brings. Let us rejoice and be glad in it.

Questions for Discussion

1. Is there a Christian strategy for change? If so, what are its ingredients? If not, how can we develop such a strategy?
2. How can we protect personhood during change, especially if we emphasize efficiency?
3. To whom are we accountable as we engage in change?
4. How can we be true to the past without being bound to it?

2 pluralism

The ads are changing on TV. In the past, most commercials showed white folks enjoying the good life. Now a variety of persons—blacks, whites, Orientals and others—smilingly talk about the virtues of various types of coffee, wax, automobiles or whatever. By using different types of people, commercials are selling to a host of audiences rather than only one group.

This shift from directing sales to a singular public to the inclusion of a larger public has not taken place overnight. It has been a result of struggle, soul searching and economic research, recognizing that people have money to buy things.

The 1954 decision of the Supreme Court to desegregate society was a trigger for a pluralism that propelled us through the 1960's. This pluralism will characterize the next quarter of a century and will greatly influence personal as well as organizational actions. We have discovered and will continue to discover that youth are both seen and heard. Women are speaking out with a new kind of independence and accomplishment. Minorities are increasingly evident in public and business, a fact that not many people predicted even a few years ago.

Some people look at these changes and say the world is in a state of decay. Others say it is all mixed up. Perhaps "mixed up" is the best description. The world is indeed a mixture of people, ideas, hopes and expectations. It is a world of many options, opportunities, contradictions and limitations, a world that is adolescent in its self-understanding.

Pluralism is a way of saying that there is more than one way to live. In fact, it goes further and says there is more than one race, one sex, one ideology, one culture, one religion, one set of doctrines. To accept other ideas as good is to recognize diversity in God's creation and to echo his blessing that "it is good."

Pluralism is as much a state of mind as anything else. The world has known for centuries that there are varieties of peoples, cultures, beliefs and institutions. What the leaders of the world have not acknowledged is that pluralism must be dealt with by allowing all people to have rights and privileges that only leaders have enjoyed.

Acceptance of pluralism means that a new level of understanding has been reached. To be sure, that understanding has come with pain and has produced new hurts. As much as some wish it had not come, the new understanding of pluralism has been a direct result of the agitation of people and groups demanding justice and new opportunities. The full recognition of the need and desirability of pluralism has yet to come and may never take place, but even our present partial recognition has produced significant and far-reaching changes.

The list of "agitators," past and present, includes Martin Luther King, Jr. in civil rights, Angela Davis in freedom of education, Ralph Nader in consumer affairs, Jack Anderson in freedom of the press and responsible government and the many critics of the Kent State shooting, Watergate and the Warren Commission report. The list grows as agitation moves into the local scene. Even some of our neighbors are involved in protests and pressure tactics to get things changed.

Similar pressures have hit the churches. Women's groups are no longer willing to raise money for good causes and allow male-dominated boards to decide where that money is going to be spent. Blacks, Hispanics and other minorities are asking that they not be overlooked, or dealt with as groups but as human beings with differences between them. The elderly have begun to make demands. In fact, the number of groups making demands increases with each passing year.

Some people are distressed that so many such groups are organized and given time to speak before church boards. "These people have had their say before. Why can't they let us get on with our business?" is a common refrain heard in the church. The people who make this statement fail to understand that everyone has a stake in the business of the church. Special interest groups appear because they are somehow affected by the decisions and actions the church makes and takes. If people are to be affected, they have a right, an obligation, to make their voices heard, and the church has a precedent in the example of Jesus Christ to provide such a hearing.

Diversity is a positive force in society and in the church for several reasons. One is that diversity allows for the surfacing of ideas and concerns that can spark new ways of acting and thinking. The most obvious pressures have come from women and blacks. Their presence in church meetings has raised questions about elections, about reporting actions to the membership, about investing church funds and being involved in social action. They have made a difference.

11

Perhaps it is a knowledge that they will continue to make a difference that promotes fear among church persons. When the church is going along on an even keel, getting enough money to keep up with its bills and operating a program that meets the needs of its leaders, then from the perspective of many members change is not desirable. At this point, the women and the blacks have added a new element. They have pushed the church to consider the "people," the majority of church members who are never heard from or who have no voice in church decsions.

Pluralism Can Be Painful

Churches that have experimented with pluralism have gone through periods of adjustment painful to some persons and groups. Yet they have also discovered that introducing diversity into their life has broadened their understanding. Different points of view have been shared in a setting of mutual concern and fellowship. New approaches to mission involvement through broadened volunteer programs, new appreciation of the conditions of life for minorities with a consequent incorporation of minorities in the life of the church, and new understandings of the needs of the elderly are examples of what happens when diversity is taken seriously. Each of these new emphases has meant that something else had to be cut back. However, these cut-backs were done in a setting of mutuality which was new in the life of these congregations.

One danger in seeking to develop diversity and be open to pluralism is that there may not be a common context or purpose that can bring people to settle on a common strategy. A failure to agree generally results from lack of openness in discussions or an inability or unwillingness on the part of the participants to listen to each other. If these are to be overcome, all must be forewarned of the danger and develop the skills to diagnose and work through obstacles.

A second benefit of diversity is the increased possibility of innovation. People with different world views (Chapter 3) come to and act on the same situation differently. As they interact in a situation of mutual concern, these persons can develop common understandings and strategies for dealing with this and other situations.

A local church was going through its planning process for the next year. One major facet of its program was to be witnessing. While there was much disagreement as to the meaning of the term, it was fully agreed that in its purest form, witnessing was being concerned enough about people to begin to treat them with respect and understanding. This insight was a result of the efforts of people with different points of view to find a common ground upon which to develop a church program, They were able to put together guidelines for their church because they were willing to listen and learn together.

While for many churches this definition is too vague and unworkable, for the congregation in question it was a new step in their understanding of the church. They had not been able to define it so precisely before. They had created a new dream, an innovation in life.

It is this type of newness that can result when diversity is allowed to affect the normal tasks and goals of the church. People come at the issues of evangelism, worship, stewardship and witnessing with different backgrounds and expectations. As the issues are worked out in an atmosphere of openness and honesty, the diversity of world views and meanings will surface. Then the church and its members gain new insights about others as well as about themselves.

Of course, tensions and misunderstandings created in such situations can polarize the church. Looking at tensions and misunderstandings as a phase in the deliberations is a helpful way to work through them to a new basis of mutuality. When it looks as if polarization might occur, the church can look to outside resources to help it through difficult times. (A fuller discussion is found in Chapter 6.)

Pluralism can be used to develop creativity in at least three other ways. It can become a form of discipline, it can help a church develop an "open style" of thought and action and it can help the church develop good and sensitive leaders. But none of these changes will take place just because there is diversity in the church. They must be worked at by church leaders to make them happen.

Pluralism as Discipline

One of the results of the developing consciousness of minorities, women and youth is the establishment of the "quota" system in the church. This is a group of rules spelling out how many leaders and employees of various organizations will be black, Spanish-speaking, women and/or youth. Based upon the percentage of members who have these characteristics, the quota system tries to ensure a mixture in leadership similar to that in the membership, thus guaranteeing diversity.

As this system has been used in the church, leaders have made efforts to find persons who can fulfill two or more of the quota requirements. For example, a young black or Spanish-speaking woman meets at least two of the requirements of most church quota systems. Sometimes such an attempt is based upon the limited finances of the church, but it can also be a ploy to limit the influence of diverse points of view.

Members of church boards tend to feel that they are the elected *representatives* of the membership, even though they often represent only a part of it. A quota system, while not a desirable long-term strategy, attempts to *require* a church council to be more representative of the members it serves.

The quota system sometimes has poor results. People are chosen because of accidents of birth, more than for who they are and what they can contribute to the life of the church, and some charge that competence is now being overshadowed by birth characteristics. This is a part of the disruption and pain caused by a conscious effort to introduce diversity into the total life of the church. Yet in spite of its limitations, the quota system seems to be the best means for ensuring short-term change in the leadership make-up of churches.

The system is also based upon an inherent logic. For example, women argue that if the church is composed of 55 percent women, 55 percent of the leaders should be women. This is a rather hard argument to dispute, although it has been ignored successfully for years. With the introduction of the quota system in local churches by action of denominational conferences and conventions, the trend is toward a much higher female representation.

This same logic will change the professional leadership of the church during the next few years. Not only is the selection of members of denominational boards and agencies a target of reformers, but the employee mix is also at issue. This means that the ordination and placement of pastors will be under the microscope of minority groups and women. These persons are demanding, with justification, that the church, denominationally and locally, reexamine its attitudes about pastoral placement especially as this relates to women. Women want to be pastors charged with as much freedom to move as men now have. The effects will be far-reaching at all levels of the church.

Pluralism has produced these pressures. Changes that result from these pressures would probably not have come so quickly or be spread so widely without the development of group feelings and a sophisticated use of group power during the past few years. A person can view these changes from any moral position. Only hindsight, however, can really give a clue as to the total long-range positive or negative effects of the pressures.

We can be sure that these pressures will be increased in the future, and it is safe to predict that change will accelerate. Therefore, the church must deal with the process of change caused by pluralism as creatively as any other reformation. This is not to deny the dislocation of people, insecurity during periods of transition and loss of status for many. It is to affirm that as parts of God's creation we will be useful in helping this world become a bit more humane.

Pluralism and Openness

The era of computers has provided us with new ways of talking and thinking. Many of us know the difficulties of getting incorrect charge records straightened out and, at the other extreme, the tremendous facilities of computers that put astronauts on the moon. These same computers have encouraged us to think in "systems" terms. The systems [1] concept enables us to look at a church in its totality. All the forces that bear upon it from its members, from the community, from auxiliaries and from the world can be looked at in detail and measured for impact.

Systems analysis helps church leaders chart the forces pushing and pulling them as a church. It also helps them to identify the various persons and groups to which the church must direct its attention and programs.

There are two types of systems: closed and open. In the closed system, information about the world and members comes from a few selected persons. They influence leaders to design programs which are then disbursed for members to consume.

The open system functions like the nerve endings on a person's skin. Input or stimuli are received from many different sources. These are received, categorized, judged and acted upon by those in charge, and several possible alternatives are tested before final action is taken.

The closed system has often been seen in churches where "influential people" really ran the church. These persons got their influence because of money, articulateness, history in the congregation or performance. The church depended on them, along with the pastor, to act as a sort of closed group. The resulting programs and emphases were generally reactions to the needs and desires of these people rather than stimuli for creative efforts to address issues and events shaping people's lives. When the programs attempted to be innovative, they were either so far ahead of the thinking of the members or so far behind their needs that the members were alienated.

1. Footnotes on page 96.

Yet, the system did function efficiently in that decisions were made and actions resulted.

The demands of pluralism are aimed at creating an open system in the church. This means that the people for whom programs are being designed feel that they should have a great deal to say about what needs are being met and how the programs meet those needs. This is a dramatic and a traumatic shift. It has caused pain and a great deal of rethinking in the church. This pain and the uncertainty that goes with it have affected all members of the church, although the demands from groups are generally directed at leaders in the churches. After all, leaders are the most visible and they make final decisions about resources and programs.

An open system requires more than a change in the attitudes of leaders. It requires that all the members confront the issues raised by pluralism. It means that such issues as changing nomination and election procedures in church councils, opening decisions to a wide range of persons and using female and minority pastors must be worked at by all members of the church. An open system cannot work if only one part of it is picked out as needing to be open. By its very definition, open refers to the entire structure of the church.

Electing women as pastors of local churches ought to have parallels in electing them to the presidency of church boards and trustees. Minority leadership in the local church is as important as having minority persons as leaders at other levels of the church.

Open deals with the way decisions are made and ideas considered. The phrase, "We will take it under advisement," has often been a way of keeping a closed system intact. Openness is possible only when all segments of the church that will be affected by decisions are sure to have some input regarding those decisions before they are made.

Pluralism and Leadership

Perhaps the most far-ranging effect of pluralistic demands is that leadership in the church will need to be better in the future. It is rather easy to tolerate mediocrity in a closed system. People who are ineffective can be hidden and by-passed when necessary, and their ineffectiveness can be camouflaged by the inner circle of decision makers.

An open system with its many windows and entrances does not allow ineffectiveness to be protected so much. It is like lifting the shades in a house to catch the gleam and promise of sunlight. The inner workings of an open system are exposed to its members.

The kind of person selected as a leader in an open and pluralistic system is very important to that system's ability to function. The leader must be skilled in negotiations, in dealing with conflict in an open and even manner, in the ability to act deliberately and considerately rather than running about at every whim of the largest giver and in involving many people in the decision making processes. Such persons are hard to find because the church has neither looked for nor trained that kind of leader in the past. While the few who now exist are looked upon as experts, in a few years most local church leaders will need to have these capacities.

In the past, the leadership has often been dependent upon the authority of a position. Bishop, pastor, chairperson of the trustees or church council carried with the titles a certain respect and authority. This is not so much the case now, nor will it be in the future. Leadership will have authority as the ability of an individual is used to bring together people in their understanding of issues and problems and then help them devise solutions that make sense and can be supported. A recent conversation with a bishop elicited a comment: "People think I have power but I really don't. I have influence, but it is up to me to see that that influence is used. I am not an authority figure just because I am bishop."

In addition to elected leaders are those who arise for or during occasions of need. When the need is over, many of these persons give up leadership and become followers again. This type of leadership will come to the surface more often in an open than in a closed situation. The ability to let people take over in an area of their competence during a particular time is an attribute of an open system. A danger is that such leaders will be required to continue after they feel that their task has been completed.

Some people just do not want to be leaders for a long time. They do not like the glamor, the responsibilities, the time demands of leadership. The open system allows people to take over for a time and then get out of leadership. This type of flow-through leadership, if it is encouraged, can take some of the strain off continuing leaders and give them a breather. As one leader recently remarked: "Me? I'm going to sit back for a spell and let you do some work. You're better at it than I am. I will get some time off. I'll be ready to take over when you're done."

Pluralism is with us for a good while. It is in our best interest as individuals and as the church to look at it as a positive redirection of God's creation and to find ways of using it creatively.

Questions for Discussion

1. What experiences have you had with the phenomenon of diversity in the church?
2. What are some long-term alternatives to a quota system?
3. How can pluralism be used to provide innovative ideas in your church?
4. Pluralism seems to make us protect our own way of doing things. Have you noticed this in yourself? How can we be more open to the points of view of others while holding on to our own beliefs?
5. Does your church have an open or a closed system?
6. How can your church prepare leadership in the light of the discussion of this chapter?

3 world views

What is a world view? It is a person's outlook on life, the framework within which a person views self and others. A world view is a mixture of the training, experiences, hopes and expectations a person has of self and others.

As a small boy, I got a great thrill from riding in our car to the closest town. The trip was only six miles and the town had less than 2,000 residents. My normal world, however, was a little community with 75 residents. Seldom did we use the car, for we could walk to every part of the community in a short while. In addition, our relatives came there often for supplies and to visit. Thus, my world view was somewhat limited.

Excursions into town were exciting—they brought new experiences to an otherwise simple existence. I was transported into another world and found the stimulation satisfying as well as somewhat fearsome.

Similar sensations of excitement, movement and interest occur even now when I travel because there are other worlds to feel, hear and touch. The trips may be thousands of miles and may be by air. Also part of my world is the auto, used to commute to work. Yet another contrast to those early days is the size of place where I work—one of the largest cities in the world.

These changes in my world have taken place over less than four decades. My perceptions of life, time and purpose have changed tremendously. In no way is my present world recognizable as issuing from my early experiences. Yet my changing world is no different from many other people's world changes. As we live so we change.

These changes in myself have not taken place because of my efforts. In many ways they were reactions to the social changes about me. During the past four decades social and economic conditions have changed drastically, three major and several minor wars have been fought, television has become a commonplace, commercial air travel has become a necessity for many businesses and space flights have been undertaken so often that we scarcely pay attention. All these and many other technological and social changes have been triggers to personal and corporate change.

19

This complex of changes, including the stimulants to social life caused by militancy among youth, women and minorities, has shaken the foundations of our thought and action patterns. We are not the persons of society we sometimes think we are. The changes have been so complete, it is difficult to remember that we did not really feel and act this way a few years ago. As we travel, it is hard to imagine that we did not travel just a few years ago. Neither did we have television in color, telephones without operators, automatic dishwashers or automobiles for nearly every family.

These changes really mean that the world views of the entire society have changed. Norms and standards of conduct are different for our children than they were for us. Our children live with a completely different set of experiences, hopes and expectations than we did at the same age. In fact, they are building their world views as we reconstruct ours.

In the midst of this sea of change there are stalwart efforts to retain the old, whether a custom, an idea, a place, an item or a practice. People need to cling to the old and the familiar in spite of seeing the need to change. It is like the preacher in a Southern Illinois town speaking out on the sin of watching television and then buying one just to see how sinful it really was. The new is enticing but the old is comfortable.

The tendency to cling to the old in spite of seeing the need for the new is known as culture lag. While this term was first used by a sociologist named Ogburn to describe the reactions to technological change, it applies just as well to social and spiritual life. We all have parts of our lives where we cultivate such lags. They give us a sort of historical reference and connection with our previous life. At time these lags keep us from realistically facing the amount of change encountered by us and by others.

This narrowness, or effort to maintain a part of the past, is most vivid for me when I return home for visits. It is always a shock to discover that the people who knew me years ago have not changed their image of me.

This can be explained easily. The people in that town had no connection with me during the formative experiences away from them. I am still "Noel's boy" or "Johnny's cousin" or some other referent which is concrete, linked to them and makes sense to them. If they talk about the present it is always with a question, "Exactly what do you do?" which can be translated to mean, "Who are you?"

A different explanation of the same events is that the world views of the people with whom I grew up and my world views are quite different. Our worlds are not the same. A tie

20

remains because of the experiences, values and ideas about life and the future we shared two decades ago. That tie is reinforced by memory, kinship and infrequent social encounters. Beyond these general ties, however, we live, think and feel in worlds separated by differing experiences, training and social expectations. We may be together but we are still apart.

The differences among people are found in more than our outlook on life. We also vary in our capacity to accept and tolerate diversity and to adapt to new situations. While all of us have developed these capacities to some extent, the differences between us remain. They remain because during our past we learned to be open, defensive, rejecting or hostile to change. The capacity to change and to tolerate diversity is as much a part of our world view as it is a piece of our total life framework.

The ability to adapt and tolerate diversity is sometimes called sophistication. Sophistication is the finesse to confront unusual situations with little or no visible discomfort. A sophisticated individual is a person who has been exposed to a wide variety of situations and has learned to handle his or her emotions with little overt display.

A person generally uses the term sophistication to praise another. It has a slang synonym, "cool." Yet, sophistication in this day and age may be more restrictive than helpful. People need to share honestly and openly of themselves, including their emotions, and such sharing is often hindered by the societal demand for sophistication. The encounter movement, which has gained popularity during the past few years, is one attempt to put sophistication in its place and free people from its restrictiveness.

While the stereotypes of city slicker and country bumpkin have been modified since I was a boy, they still characterize extremes of sophistication. In a society such as ours, and within the church, both are needed. At times there needs to be an aloofness toward situations, but at other times there must be an outpouring of human empathy and emotion. The skill of a church to help people do each at the proper time is a resource to be coveted and developed.

Loose Ends

The commonality of life shared by people in the church is sometimes confounded by their desire to maintain their sophistication. People need a solid basis for their lives. The church through its worship, teaching and fellowship can provide such a basis. In spite of changing world views, and in spite of the variations in these world views, the need to tie that world view to a base of belief and value is universal.

The main theme of *Why Conservative Churches Are Growing*[1] by Dean Kelley is that people need to have a base of belief that demands something from them. They need discipline with purpose. When they find that in a church, they join and participate. The same theme was sounded in *Punctured Preconceptions*,[2] where it was identified as a need for developing a valid meaning system.

It is impossible for people to become so sophisticated that they do not need a stability based upon a meaningful purpose in life. They can be inhibited from finding that purpose by a church that emphasizes a sophisticated approach to life and the world. Such a church fails in its basic mission to call people to God in Jesus Christ.

One needs only to read the paper to learn of people who take their own lives because they have no purpose in living. The man who recently survived a jump from the Golden Gate Bridge in San Francisco said, "I didn't have any reason to live." The same sentiment was echoed by a former POW who reported that "Two men died because they did not have any reason to live."

The world has gotten smaller; we know more about other people; we see more of other cultures. We listen with an almost casual air of unconcern to requests for help from people trapped in life situations. We are not startled by poverty, cruelty or deprivation. We are sophisticated. Yet, in spite of the desire to keep our cool, we are at loose ends. We have difficulty in sorting out any underlying purpose in our life that would give it meaning and direction.

Added to this personal dilemma is the fact that the church has not helped us in the sorting process, nor has it even been able to provide us with guidelines to help us build meaning. Indeed, the church has often been a hindrance.

Why can the church not help us? Two major reasons stand out. The first is polarization within the church, which greatly affects communication and sharing between people. The second reason is the frustration of articulate people, skilled in the church to the point where they withdraw before creative exchange and dialogue can be established. It is worthwhile for us to look at both of these reasons.

Polarization

Polarization has become a popular word because it represents an easily identifiable situation in many churches. Polarization takes place when people are unable to communicate.

Its cause is not that people hold different points of view but that individuals are unable to talk together about their divergent feelings.

Polarization occurs because of emotional reactions and the defenses against these reactions. Sophistication, the ability to control one's emotions as well as an awareness of various types of social stimuli, has not helped us overcome polarization. Sophistication has not enabled people to deal rationally with emotional topics such as race, poverty and doctrine. It has enabled us to be a bit more devious.

Polarization can be precipitated over almost anything. It takes shape when people begin to identify themselves in two opposing camps—a "we-they" situation. Former community organizer Saul Alinsky used such situations for group advantage. In fact, he felt that the only way for poor people to get themselves organized effectively was to have a collective enemy. This enemy (landlord, unfair merchant, city planner) gave the individualized, disorganized and exploited community residents a symbol to defeat. They could then rally together to fight the enemy.

Alinsky's tactic was to develop "we-they" situations for the purpose of creativity. This was polarization with a purpose, and it tended to be controlled carefully by the community organizers. Once a situation got out of control the person in power could legitimately use force to overcome the community people. It is this latter point that is often lost on the church. Creativity in polarization can take place only when there is control on both sides of the issue.

Churches generally function without the benefit of a person with Alinsky's talents. They often polarize around issues of no import. One church in a large city, with many opportunities for mission, had a major problem deciding which color to use in the lavatories.

Opportunities for polarization may increase dramatically during the next few years. One contributing reason is mobility, which brings together persons with widely divergent world views. They find themselves in the same congregation attempting to define the mission of the church.

Take the case of one church in Connecticut. The community is one in which the social and intellectual pace have been those of a small industrial town. Ethnic groups predominate and the style of life is relatively slow and unpretentious. Many townspeople have not been to New York City, about a ninety-minute trip, nor to many of the other communities in Connecticut. The world views of many residents are limited.

Into this community has moved a contingent of airline personnel, along with a number of middle management personnel of industries locating north of New York City. The new residents have generally had college backgrounds and are used to money and travel. They are comfortable being on the move, having resources at their disposal, deciding and acting.

These two groups of people, the natives and the new residents, have world views and life expectations as different as night and day. Yet they belong to the same church. They are trying to develop a communication pattern that will enable them to talk meaningfully about the church's mission in their community and in the world. It is easy for an outsider to see how the varying understandings of life held by these groups generate animosity. The natives often use "We have always done it this way" as an argument against the innovations suggested by the newcomers, a defensive posture that produces hostile frustration in the newcomers.

This example might be just as true in Illinois or Iowa or the suburban rings around cities in Michigan, Florida, Texas or California. Mobility throughout the world brings people with divergent points of view and world views into the same fellowship with little warning or time for preparation. Once there, they must all begin to deal with pluralism. A perceptive church will seek help to guide them through such periods.

Frustration

Radical acts are generally committed or masterminded by persons who have benefitted enough from societal rewards to believe that they can attain still more rewards. One failure of the philosophy of Karl Marx is his lack of recognition that a working class which sees no opportunity for ever sharing in the rewards of society will have little incentive to revolt. It is only when there are visible opportunities for material or physical advancement that persons are willing to vent their frustration on the system.[3]

The same is true in the church. People who have little hope of making the church receptive to their needs will leave. They may try some radical act before they go to test the possibility of introducing change. If the test fails they will go; if the test is a partial success they will try again. Eventually, however, frustration produces alienation and a giving up.

The other side of the coin in equally valid. People who tolerate rapid and complete change also become frustrated and leave. Their frustration comes from a different source, the church's inability to maintain stability and purpose in the face of change. They are also against gradual change because they see it as eroding their institution.

24

It is difficult to provide a middle ground that will protect personhood and allow transition. This is particularly true when people on the council are strong in their convictions. This should not be a deterrent, however, since the most stimulating persons in church councils are those who raise hard questions. They seem like thorns in the side and are often viewed as obstructionists. When such persons leave, however, creativity is greatly diminished.

A church in New England was involved in a program to combat racism. The leader of the program, a dedicated, somewhat liberal woman, tried hard to get people to engage in dialogue with persons of other races. She met only resistance. Finally she left the church. Two years later, after a meeting to evaluate the program, members of the church council told her that since she had left they had not had to think creatively or even to think at all about the problem of race. They did not like the situation even though they had brought it about through their collective disregard and ridicule.

Frustration sets in when people are not allowed to express their world views. They feel caught in an iron straight jacket that locks them into habits and thought patterns from their past. They feel like grown children who must dress like babies. It is ridiculous and impossible.

Frustration and polarization tend to immobilize people, to drain energies through tension and conflict. People begin to feel that perhaps they are wrong and a bit confused. Yet they cannot admit this feeling—to do so would then allow the opponent to win. Instead, they appear to go on with their daily routines totally convinced that they are right and others are wrong. They must always maintain an air of sophistication.

These silent desperations—wanting to make contact with others but feeling that such contact will only produce pain— have greatly inhibited the ability of individuals to develop meaning bases. A meaning system and purpose for life must be continually tested and revised through interaction with others who are trusted and respected. When such trust and respect do not exist, one becomes focused upon oneself and thus dies somewhat toward the very persons who could both help and be helped.

The church is the one place where new steps in dialogue building can take place—but that has not happened. It might, just possibly, happen in the future, and we will look at that possibility to gain a new perspective on the potentialities and problems inherent in the changing world views in our own lives and in the church.

New Possibilities and New Problems

1. We should respect others even though we do not agree with their approach or interpretation of life. There is much being written about changing life styles in love, sex and marriage. In many cases, these proposals are "far out" from the perspectives of most people in the church. Even so, we should be free enough to discuss our differences openly and with some attempt to understand each other's positions.

Two young pastors were talking recently, and one asked the other how his marriage was going. He replied that he and his wife were not doing so well. In fact, he said, it had gotten to the point where they were writing notes rather than talking to each other. This brought the reaction, "Gee, that's how bad it is?" to which the other minister explained, "I sat down and told her all the things I had been feeling and she took them the wrong way." This minister apparently felt that his wife was really incapable of talking on his level.

How often each of us has been in a similar situation where we have been talked down to or over by someone. What kinds of feelings does this arouse? They may be described variously, but the essence is distaste. A superior attitude hastens lack of communication and, within organizations, disaster.

If we learned anything during the years of McCarthy with his innuendos, the John Birch Society which looks at every rock with suspicion, and the national administrations with their lack of honesty, we should have learned that understanding is built through honest and open interchange. Understanding is a sharing of experiences. It is not being coy or cute. It involves respect for the other person.

This does not mean that we must approve of the opinions, actions or desires of others. It does mean that we must try to "live where the other person lives" in order to get perspective on the forces pushing others to do what they do.

This is particularly true in the church, where we deal with people's ultimate emotions. Interpretations of death and purposes for living are not easy subjects to discuss. Often people downgrade the ideas and opinions of others in order to protect their own identity and philosophy. The person doing the downgrading is really in need of help and understanding, but is often most unwilling to accept it.

A layman worked long and hard for the church. He taught church school, served on the church council, was a member of the trustees and could be counted upon to assist in the various social and service activities of the church. Yet it was impossible to talk to him in a rational manner about race.

Invariably, he would assume a superior attitude of knowledge about blacks and others. He was cruel and sarcastic to those who wanted to discuss the issue.

Such persons are found in most churches, often holding positions of influence and leadership. They cannot understand other points of view because they never allow themselves the thrill of getting to know other people. They put themselves behind defensive walls.

This is not a new problem, but it takes on new dimensions with sophistication. People who do not want to understand are very subtle in redirecting conversations or double talking around issues. They are clever in the use of cliches that arouse emotion and defeat dialogue. They have learned how to control the situation—or they leave.

One task of the church is to help such persons learn respect. This can be done by allowing them to serve on small committees with those who hold different viewpoints. The techniques suggested in Chapter 6 can also be used. Underlying all these efforts should be a reexamination of the meaning of the gospel.

2. A mixture of people with divergent world views contains the possibility for developing a wide variety of interest groups. People with particular interests may be drawn together around specific issues or common skills. For instance, a group of men became interested in educating teenagers in the art of using radio in the church. Some of the men were technicians; some were interested in radio as a hobby. They pooled their interests and made creative use of them for the church.

Interest groups bring people together for specific activities and personal sharing, and the atmosphere of an interest group can be a prelude to deeper communication. If some members of a church belong to two or more such groups, a network of communication can be developed.

People communicate because they learn to trust each other. Trust begins in the nonemotional areas of life. In this sense, the more possibility there is for mutual sharing through interest groups in the church, the more likelihood there is that a fellowship will be developed.

One problem with interest groups is that they can become exclusive cliques. Members develop their own verbal codes and often distinctive types of attire. They find their identity in the church through the interest group, which then takes on the character of a permanent—and exclusive—organization.

Interest groups should be short-lived. In our mobile society the membership changes even if the group does not, and the specific reason for initiating a group passes with shifts in members, the church and the society.

A basic difficulty with groups is that they tend to forget their reason for being. They just go on, revising their activities without reexamining their purpose. For example, a woman's group in a church began to roll newspapers for a moving firm to make money for a mission project. These women continued to meet three years later, although each of them felt that the meeting time was bad, the task boring and the mission project was funded. They did not know how to quit.

Interest groups should be flexible enough to allow their members to leave, and they should not be built exclusively around certain people. People should not be saddled with responsibilities beyond their interests. Yet a person who initiates a project is often permanently fixed in that group by image. This should not be, especially when diversity in the church promises many opportunities for involvement. It is not beneficial to people to be stuck with a group they have outgrown.

3. Differing world views provide exciting opportunities for developing new programs and a variety of experiences. It is much more interesting to have someone who has been to a mission station tell about it than to read a letter or watch a movie about it. In this world and in the church, the number of persons with such experience is increasing rapidly. VISTA volunteers can provide new insights to local church members. Women with experience in the women's liberation movement can give new meaning to dialogue around the issues of justice and oppression. Such people abound in the churches and represent a relatively untapped source of insight.

One of the most promising aspects of this age is the opportunity to interact with people who have other histories. We can easily approach diversity with positive, creative expectations. This is a better approach than to remain an ingrown group with a comfortable but stifling set of traditions. Our minds can be stretched, our insights enriched by exchanging ideas and concepts with persons who can talk and feel meaningfully the issues of life to which faith can make response. We can confront those with non-Christian beliefs and be challenged. Such interchanges have a tremendous potential for adding an enriched perspective and a new vigor to our familiar ways of doing, thinking and feeling.

This does not mean that people and churches should be like straws in the wind. The church has a foundation and purpose that should include diversity, but it also has a singleness of mind. Each church has its own heritage and its distinctive mark. These should not be hidden. The church is a combination of prophet and sinner, working together to make it a distinctive human-divine venture of faith.

Personal and church identity are possible only when a person feels worth in what he or she has been or now is. It is true that identity can be transformed into a rigid pride which is outgrown by all others except a small group. The Flat World Society, for instance, continues in this era of space exploration. And churches often find themselves in the same situation. They feel they minister to families, but their worshipping congregation is composed mainly of widows. They think of themselves as a church of aristocrats, but exist in a poverty area.

The new possibilities of mixing a variety of world views in the church hinge upon the attitudes we bring to such a mix. If we are apprehensive and defensive, our identity may be threatened and we may resort to rolling newspapers because that is what we started out to do many years ago. On the other hand, if we are willing to listen, think and talk with persons from different backgrounds, experiences and commitments, we can become creative and exciting both as persons and as churches.

Questions for Discussion

1. What are some of the changes that have taken place in your world view? What do you attempt to hold to in spite of everything?
2. How has sophistication assisted your church in understanding its mission? How has it been a liability?
3. Does your church help you pull together the loose ends of life into a meaningful belief system? If not, why not?
4. How do you deal with polarization in your church?
5. How do you gauge the level of frustration in your church? What do you do about it?
6. Which of the three possibilities discussed in the last part of the chapter make most sense for your church? Why? What others can you think of that were not discussed?

4 owners and participants

People want to "own" things. They are possessive. They like to use the words "mine" and "yours." They talk about property and propriety as *theirs*.

This emphasis on "my" is one way people express their identity and status. It may also be a reflection of an abiding selfishness in the nature of humans, and it certainly appears to be a well-nigh universal human trait.

Ownership is a big word. Translated into the language of the church it refers to leaders, to buildings or to special spots of real estate. "This is my church!" "This is my pastor." "They are my people." "My church owns that land." Such common phrases convey a great deal of meaning, and members and nonmembers alike understand them.

These phrases convey emotional as well as factual information. They speak of ownership. Ownership may only be verbal, but even in this sense there is purpose, identity and status for the users of the words.

Even verbal meanings may be translated into actual ownership at times. A church some years ago received a bequest from a person who had lived only a block away. The unusual aspect of the bequest was that the man had never been on the church rolls, had not attended and was unknown to the pastor and most leaders. He willed money to the church because of what it stood for in the community. It was a part of his life and he wanted to express his ownership of its image and influence.

The use of the words "my" and "mine" and "ours" and "theirs" lets people know where they stand with regard to other people, institutions and ideas. This is true regardless of the context. For example, a parallel to church usage is the more intimate descriptions of "my" husband or wife, children, home, job, car, boss, hobby and so forth.

All of the my's a person feels and expresses make up the totality of that person. All of the my's, your's, our's, and their's constitute a total social setting. Without these references to identity and status, people could not identify themselves, their friends or their enemies. These are also ways people and churches reflect upon their past, present and future. The points of personal ownership by members and nonmembers provide the context for describing the church.

This personal image of life is an extremely important concept for the church. The "myness" of members, pastors and nonmembers ought to be viewed positively rather than treated as a mistake. It should be recognized as a way we humans think about our lives. Each my or mine, ours or theirs, speaks of personal and church goals, hopes, habits, thoughts and activities. They are a mix of history and tradition, expectation and purpose, hope and desire. Without the my there is no I, and people without an identity are little good to anyone including themselves.

One of the consequences of increased pluralism and the mixing of world views in the church is an increased desire on the part of many people to demand more say in the decisions that affect them. This means that they want to have more influence over the way programs are begun and run. This might be illustrated by an exchange with a lay person regarding a specific program.

"Why did your church get involved in this program?"

"I don't know." (pause) "I guess it's because we are good Methodists." (another pause) "Now, just why *did* we?"

He then began to probe in his mind some of the possible reasons for the program and the involvement of their local church. His consciousness had been raised.

When their consciousness is raised, people begin to ask the reasons for doing things. When they cannot find adequate and satisfying answers to their inquiries, they get the feeling of being used. "Someone decided for us and we just did it with no strong feeling one way or the other. It seemed like a normal thing to do." Our ways of acting and thinking are natural until someone alerts us to the fact that there may be no good reason for them.

Unless we are prodded, many of us do not raise the "why" question. One of the benefits of the influence of diverse world views is that more and more people are asking "why?" They feel that those who make decisions affecting them should be answerable to them, that all should own the decisions and the reasons for the decisions.

There is no crisis at this point yet. But as church people think, plan and talk together, it is becoming obvious that throughout the church people are wanting to do more talking and not just listening. The easy acceptance of ideas and suggestions is no longer the typical behavior of laity. They want a piece of the action. They want to be heard as well as to hear.

How can such two-way communication take place frequent-

ly and effectively? Some people will say the only requirements are a good attitude, a comfortable setting and a
common topic. This is the old country store image of communication, where people gathered to exchange gossip and be
comfortable with friends. But aside from the fact that there
are few country stores, much evidence has been accumulated
to show that honest communication is not so simple.

The surroundings or the trappings do not guarantee communication. Neither do the techniques of mass media. It is more
likely to take place where there is a commonness of purpose, a
freedom to be inspired by another and a willingness to share
emotions. Communication does not occur by word, picture or
feeling alone. It is all of these. In the church, people feel a
great need for deeper sharing of common purpose, inspiration
and emotion.

"It's not so much getting your way in program that counts
but knowing that you count enough to be listened to."

These sentiments, expressed by a housewife in Pennsyl-
vania, get at the heart of the issue. How do leaders and the
led get to the place where this can really happen? Some observations on the issue might produce a few more attempts to
open the channels of communication. One caution; The technique or approach will need to be adapted according to the
situation.

Human Beings and Manipulation

"If you say I am a human being, then treat me like one!"

Most church leaders would get defensive with an accu-
sation like that. Most would say that they do treat people like
humans. Before we get ourselves caught in our own righteous-
ness, it would be well for us to think about how we want people involved in the church.

We want them to do jobs we have selected. We select them
to fill certain purposes we think we essential. We take into
consideration their special training and talents, and we sometimes ask them about their interests. You see, we do all the
thinking, feeling and acting. They are fitting into our agendas,
concepts and desires. Our reaction, when someone points this
out, tends to be: "We have the welfare of the church in mind.
Anyway, these seem to be the best people for the jobs." Good
defensive reactions, but the reasons are open for debate.

Too seldom do we in the church allow participation to be on
a human basis. Participation is on the basis of what the
church needs to have done in order to survive or accomplish
set goals. Those goals have often been agreed upon by a limited group of people, acting in a conscientious manner to be

sure, but a small group nevertheless. If we are interested in getting people to participate so that diversity of backgrounds and world views can provide a creative spark, we will need to revise our estimates of the kinds of jobs that are needed and can be performed to help the church minister to people. When we begin these rethinkings, we will need to include those "other" people. When we have that much courage and freedom we will have embarked on a process of change that will lead to a totally new future. There is no guarantee that the new future will be to our liking, but it may be closer to God's direction.

Four techniques can and should be used by the church to get more people involved in its program and decisions. These are (1) the use of nonthreatening but provocative ways to expose the interests and feelings of people toward the church; (2) a conscious effort on the part of the leaders in the church to seek out the new persons, the disenchanted members and the nonvocal persons to find out what they are saying; (3) a redefinition of the kinds of tasks needed in the church; and (4) making certain that what can be done is valid and useful to people and within the confines of the purposes of the church. The techniques are attempts to develop a manner of participation that emphasizes human fulfillment over institutional maintenance.

These techniques cannot be easily applied in all churches. They are difficult. There appear to be no alternatives, however, if the church wishes to retain and regain vitality and involvement from many people. The desire to own the church in a very personal and creative manner is more forcefully expressed each passing year.

Strain Between the Leaders and the Led

In a recent international survey of church members and pastors, more than 60 percent of the laity said they wanted more say in decisions affecting them. What do they mean? They want to have some voice in shaping the policies and developing the programs of their church. This is not the full story, however. No one is expecting leaders in any institution to go out and get a set of opinions before decisions are made. The point is that deciding what is best for someone, and expecting that person to accept the decision graciously and unquestioningly, is oppressive and paternalistic.

These are pretty hard words. Let us look at the concepts they convey. Young people rebel against parents, teachers and authority figures in general because youth need the freedom to make mistakes. This exercise of freedom is regarded as an

33

opportunity to improve upon or at least to have some influence upon their own life situations. This is the same type of freedom being requested by minority groups, women, laity and most other segments of society that feel oppressed. It is a legitimate request and needs to be taken seriously. All of us can sympathize if we will just think back to some time in our lives when we needed freedom to make decisions that greatly affected us.

Decisions imposed on people do oppress them by not allowing them to creatively interact with decision makers before decisions are made. This interaction may result in the same decision, but it just as often does not. Because of broader participation modifications are introduced into the decision and these often guarantee greater personal integrity or freedom for the people who make the decisions as well as those affected. In addition, the people most affected have had some input and the decision makers have become more aware of the new dimensions of the church.

Protectionism is a habit or an attitude that can develop all too quickly. It is expectations about one's role and those of others, rooted in a need to affirm one's own superiority.

Charity, for example, is often protective because it assumes that the giver is somehow "better" than the recipient. The system of welfare, beginning with the "poor farms" of the rural era, assumes that the unfortunate of society are somehow less worthy than the fortunate. This same attitude can be present in the church when we hire people because they need a job, lend them money or even give them a word of recommendation. All these nice and helpful gestures can be protective, if our attitudes are condescending.

In the church protectionism can extend to the search for new participants and leaders. It is communicated best by the attitude, "We have succumbed to asking you to be a part of this great enterprise." It may also be conveyed, for example, in the attitudes of a finance committee that divides money for missions or emergency appeals, or in the attitudes of a pulpit search committee as it interviews a prospective minister.

Of all the tortures imposed upon a person living in a free society and belonging to a voluntary organization, there are few so demeaning or so prevalent as protectionism. This set of attitudes takes away human dignity as quickly as does enforced capitivity. In both capitivity and protectionism, a person must admit that he or she is somehow inferior in order to receive any benefits. Five dollars from Dad may be necessary; therefore, a young person plays the game of inferiority for the sake of a short-term gain.

There comes a time, however, when sensitive and sophisticated people can no longer quietly sit by and agree to the assumptions of leaders that they know what is best for the church. We do not live in that kind of world any longer. We have a growing awareness of individual worth. While North American society was ostensibly founded upon that awareness, it has not functioned according to it. Nor has the church. The problem now appears to be, to find some means of changing the system so that people do have full participatory rights.

The strain between the leaders and the led, oppression and protectionism, will be with us for quite a while. But the strain can be lessened, and not exploited. This is very important in the church, for exploitation results in radicalism and apathy while lessening the strain can produce initiative and creativity. The latter is clearly our goal.

Reaching that goal requires patience and a lot of help. The techniques that can help are: (1) talk through the strain and attempt to gauge its intensity; (2) devise new ways of sharing responsibilities among the leaders and the followers; and (3) develop a process whereby both rewards and failures can be shared by both leaders and followers. In many ways these are costly means but the cost is more to pride than it is to a person, and in most cases the losses are temporary rather than long term. The real test is whether people are willing to take the risk of using these techniques in the church.

Many leaders have great difficulty in talking through with followers the nature of the strain that develops between them. For some reason, leaders acquire a halo just by being leaders. They appear unreachable. They are busy or at least seem to be; important and pressing items need their attention. They often appear to condescend to talk to followers, or in the case of aldermen in some cities to speak and listen to their constituents. In each case, the follower is expected to go to the leader, which means that the leader sets the time and designates the place for the interchange. All the advantages are in his favor, while the follower comes without the strong psychological backing of familiar surroundings. This one-sided situation militates against meaningful discussion.

This tendency of leaders to require followers to come to them is as common in the church as elsewhere. But it adds to the strain and reinforces the subservient attitude begun by the election to leadership. In the church, where leaders are elected volunteers attempting to interest other volunteers in giving time for specific tasks, it is out of place. A good leader in the church recognizes this and begins the process of reducing strain by attempting to meet the follower in a situation favorable to the follower. The leader goes to the led rather than vice versa.

This is no great revelation. It is just contrary to the normal tendencies of leaders. And oddly enough, such an attempt is not always welcomed by the followers; some people do not want to be sought out. Yet, if a bridge is to be built across the chasm between leaders and followers, it is incumbent upon the leader to go find the followers and talk to them where they live.

This technique has three effects for the leaders and the church. First, it begins to revise the image of untouchableness surrounding a leader. Of course, just the fact that a leader seeks out a follower does not mean the attitudes of either will be conducive to dialogue. Both must be receptive and willing to discuss a situation or issue. But if a leader takes the time and exerts the energy to search them out, people begin to see the leader is another human being.

A few years ago a denomination was faced with a financial crisis because local churches were threatening to withhold money. The issue was gifts of money by the national offices for social action. One national office, assigned the responsibility for promotion, decided to send its people out to groups of local churches around the country. They went to listen and to explain. They received much criticism but also some commendation. The financial crises was averted, and leaders in the office attribute the turnaround to the response to leaders coming to hear people where they lived.

A second effect of this approach is that the follower can be more honest in his or her part of the conversation. In familiar surroundings, a person will be more willing to expose feelings than he would be in alien territory. Ministers who visit in people's homes know that difference.

A third effect is that the integrity of the leader is recognized, and along with that, the follower may become much more willing to be involved in the program of the church. There is respect for a person who leaves his or her natural setting and seeks out others. This is very evident in political campaigns, where campaigners who get out and mingle are respected for making the effort.

Talking is fine but directing the talk to objective facts is a second part of the task. Strain is emotional. It is based on perceptions of differences in roles and worth. If talk about the strain is to be mutually beneficial, it must move from the emotional level to a discussion of facts.

Such a movement is difficult but can be based upon a rational process. The first step is to identify the kind and amount of strain that exists or is perceived to exist. What causes it to intensify or to lessen? When is it most evident? Are there persons who aggravate the situation? Are there persons who help calm troubled waters? As these kinds of questions are answered, the problem becomes pinpointed. It may also be possible to use the answers to list some possible solutions to the problem. It is always helpful to put these down on paper.

After the dimensions of the problem and the potential solutions are written down, the task becomes one of working out the most beneficial solution for all. This is a process that must be repeated frequently, not one that produces a final solution for all time. People change, situations change and with these changes, new strains and tensions are introduced.

As people focus their talk upon objective items, there will probably emerge a consensus that two needs must be met in order to lessen the strain: (1) delineation of the responsibilities of both leader and followers, and (2) the necessity for a leader to share both the failures and the rewards. According to the way these needs are met, the strain may intensify to the breaking point or it may be lessened.

One of the demands of church people is to have more say in programs. This means that they want more responsibilty for designing and implementing those programs. They are not content to let others decide what their church is to be doing. They feel that they know about situations and are willing to begin to struggle with program to meet those situations. Every church I have assisted in developing a planning and program development process has had a set of leaders who insisted that the"average" lay person cared very little about programs. As we worked at getting involvement through input and feedback, the leaders have been amazed and excited at the response and enthusiasm of members who became involved in planning and deciding upon programs.

In a recent international study, laity insisted that one of the major tasks of denominational leaders is to function as counselors to the local church. Local church members wanted full responsibility for what goes on in their church, but were asking that a person with a broad perspective and a range of experience be available to them when needed.

This clear delineation of roles carries with it responsibilities for each of the two groups. The local group has responsibility for local design and implementation, while the national group has responsibility for bringing knowledge, information and experience to bear upon problems or situations identified by local church members. When there is such a clear distinction of roles, clear responsibilities can be developed. Such clarity does not often exist because leaders too often feel that their positions should allow them to assume some of the responsibilities of the led, such as implementing or adjusting programs. Rebellion on the part of laity is an indication that the time for such overextension of roles, which tend to result in paternalism and oppression, is gone.

The other most frequent bone of contention is the sharing of rewards and failures. Leaders get the accolades, though they cannot accomplish great and wonderful things without the dedication and assistance of followers. Even when success is the result of a leader's approach, which allows more followers to assume their rightful roles and thus allow a church to function better, the leader is dependent upon the led actually doing their jobs and assuming their responsibilities.

Leaders should certainly share their accolades with the workers. Everyone likes recognition. All people need some sort of status, even in the church. People like to own success or failure just the same as the leader. In fact, when there is shared ownership of success and failure, a new spirit of unity pervades the church. Without such sharing, apathy spreads, and if there is a failure, a great deal of effort is spent trying to locate blame.

Let us recognize the obvious. The church is an organization. It is composed of people. There are leaders and followers. There is strain between these two groups in spite of their common dedication. It is possible to intensify or reduce that strain by dealing as people with people. The designation of a leader produces an image of superiority that must be broken if the atmosphere of the church is to reflect Christian fellowship. This would be hastened if the issues of responsibility, rewards and failures were worked out more carefully and more often.

Broadening the Net

One of the premises for developing broad ownership of decisions in the church is that more and more people ought to get involved. This is the dream of many pastors and the aim of most church leaders. Yet many leaders are doubtful of the ability of a large number of persons to get intelligently involved in decision-making, which often stems from their feeling that power shared is power lost.

Power is the ability to get things done. Leaders have power because people are willing to do what they ask. When people are not willing to do as leaders request, then leaders do not have power, just a position. This is especially true in the church. Thus, power requires the ability to influence and convince others that what is being done is in their best interest and fulfills the purposes of the church.

People are most convinced that their self-interest is being served when they have the opportunity to identify that self-interest and suggest the means by which it can be satisfied. And this can only happen when leaders make certain that the followers are sharers of power, that they have influence. They become a referendum body which is expected to voice its desires and is questioned about its desires frequently. Such a process is very important in this age of mobility, bringing constant mixtures of world views into our congregations.

Exposing Interests

One of the main difficulties in getting people involved is knowing exactly what their interests are. Many pastors and churches have tried interest-finder surveys and have ended up with a body of information they did not know how to use. One reason for this dilemma is that the interests listed do not fit the program offerings or needs of the church. Another problem is that the skills noted are not of such a nature that the church could make adequate use of them. If a church is going to survey interests it makes sense to begin where the church program is or hopes to be shortly, and then talk to members about their potential involvement.

It is generally awkward to approach a person and ask what he or she would be interested in doing in the church. Responses to such a question vary from the sublime to the ridiculous. It is better to focus on arousing people's involvement with an impersonal presentation that does not ask for any commitment. The nonpersonal approach, although focused on the individual, allows both the questioner and the questioned to exchange information and feelings with limited personal risk.

An example of this approach occurs often in social surveys. This was true in the North American Inter-Church Study conducted in 1971. The interviewers in this study found that the interview instrument, an objective and impersonal form that was designed to elicit feelings, attitudes and behavior, became the stimulus for getting people to talk about their own relationships to the church. To be sure, the instrument was administered by interested persons who had been trained to listen, but the fact was that over and over the interviewers reported that the interview setting produced a no-risk or a limited-risk situation for them and for the interviewees. In this setting the individuals both had freedom to be themselves.

There is a difference between doing a survey and getting

people involved in the church. The difference, however, does not involve the technique but the substance of the contact. An approach that earnestly seeks to deal with another person as an individual without any prejudgment is the key to involvement. This is true whether one is seeking participation in a church or in decisions being made within the church. It is how the subject matter is presented and the attitude of the presenter which are the real keys to success in getting people committed to become involved.

It would be wise to allow laity to systematically visit church members to secure their involvement. Better than most ministers, laity can visit without being a reminder of a lack of attendance by the persons being visited. This does not relieve the pastor of the obligation to visit. It merely opens another avenue of approach, appealing to many of the laity.

In such a visit, it is wise to focus on the hopes, plans and programs of the church, not in an attempt to sell the church but in an effort to indicate the extent of its work and activity in all spheres of human life. This provides a common subject of interest along with a presentation that is not recriminating. It has very personal implications for both persons, but there is limited personal risk for both parties. It would be obvious that the person or persons doing the presentation were interested and involved.

This is a very simple technique and pays rich dividends to those who use it. It allows people to get things off their chests about the church and its leadership and programs in a nonjudgmental setting. It meets them in their surroundings where they are more at ease and free to vent their feelings. It also allows them to say what they might do to become more involved in the church. The technique is both a lightning rod to attract dissension and a prod to let people know that the church cares and is concerned about their involvement.

Seeking Out All Members

A continuing problem in the church is the limitation of time on the part of both leaders and followers. This is particularly true when it comes to dealing with the interpersonal process of keeping people involved in the church. Church leaders tend to direct most of their energy toward those whom they know will respond positively. All leaders know that this is not the proper thing to do, but most leaders do not have time to waste on members who have shown no interest or have not been active in the church since the day they took their vows.

It is natural to be upset with people who neglect the membership duties they accepted before a congregation. The

Christian religion, and therefore the church, is not natural in the same sense. It commands us to go to those people with a new message of love and forgiveness. When a church takes such an approach toward its membership, a new spirit of fellowship and concern is born.

A church in the midwest decided that one of its goals during the next year would be to involve members who had become inactive. Teams of laity visited and encouraged. The pastor assumed new responsibilities of mediation between families and long-time enemies. Misunderstandings and slights of years standing were uncovered. At the end of the year a service of penitence, thanksgiving and celebration was held. It was held not for those who had been regained, since the number was relatively small, but for the active members who had developed a new awareness of the calling of Christ and the possibility of love and forgiveness.

While not everyone who says "Lord, Lord" will enter the kingdom, it is not for church leaders to determine which members do and which do not. It is the responsibility of the church and its leaders to try and keep all members involved. This means trying and trying and trying and. . . .

The implication is quite important. The church should make it a point to seek out the new persons, the disenchanted and the nonvocal or inactive persons to get their hearing and interest. There are reasons why people are disenchanted and nonvocal, and it is possible to discover what those reasons are. But such discoveries are not made unless one is willing to take the time and make the effort to go find people and listen to what they have to say.

Many studies of churches have shown that churches often become little social cliques run for the benefit of a few leaders and the pastor. They are closed systems. The calling of the church is to be more; it is our privilege at this time to open the system and let the Spirit speak and act in this new age.

Valid and Useful Activities

Church leaders should be under no illusions. People will become involved in the church only when they have something valid and useful to do or when the church provides meaningful and helpful services and activities. The catch, of course, is that the members who are not involved define what is valid, useful, meaningful and helpful. It is therefore necessary to go find out their definitions. However, it is not enough just to find out what they think and then what they would like to do in the church. It is essential to go the next mile and devise ways to utilize their interests and skills so that the activity has meaning for both the person and the church. No "make-work" jobs are wanted, nor are jobs that take people too far from their normal or day-by-day activities. But tasks that are essential to the church and important to the members will get people interested and involved.

Leaders often feel that their task is to educate, inform and motivate people. This is only partially true. The church is not really one group doing *for* or *to* another group. The church is a series of groups doing *with* each other. They are linked by a commonality of purposes, liturgy and history. In this sense, the church becomes the arena where people learn, do, think and worship each according to the talents and inclinations that are uniquely his or hers. If this means that some people will be cooks for suppers, some will be teachers for church school, some will be handymen for fix-ups, some will be visitors, so much the better. The church can and should use these people in their chosen fields of interest.

There is no talent too insignificant or task too humble to be useful in the work of the church. It is unfair for church leaders to feel that involvement should be limited to education, worship, age-group advisors and other like tasks. There are sewing tasks that can be used for mission work; there are clerical tasks that can gainfully use the time and energy of people of all ages; there are gardening tasks that can use creativity, patience and care. All of these might involve new people in the church. The task, however, must not be substituted for the church or for the more deeply meaningful search for relationships with God and people.

In this sense, each task done for and in the name of the church should be intertwined with some training and information, relating that task to the overarching mission and message of the church. This is a need most felt when we speak about training leaders, teachers and officers. It is clear that such persons need to be versed in the polity of the church, its organizational needs and their specific responsibilities in this particular church. It seldom occurs to church leaders that it would be helpful for volunteers other than teachers and officers to catch a glimpse of how they relate to the total message of the church, as reflected in their congregation.

How often I have gone into a church building and found no one but a custodian! What a difference that person makes to a visitor's initial impression when he or she feels a dedication to the church and what it is doing! When this happens, the custodian is no longer an employee but a witness. That is what training and information can do for people. They begin to understand how they fit into the totality of the church and that they are as important as teachers, leaders and pastors.

The plea at this point is not only to broaden the net by which people are sought but also to enrich the ways in which people can use their talents and energies for the church. Encourage people in the church to really believe that they make a difference. Provide them with opportunity to work in valid and useful ways in the programs of the church. Involve them in training so that their task and energy are used to become more Christian. Let them know what the church is doing and what part they are playing in its totality.

Participation on Human Terms

The Russell Sage Foundation has for several years been publishing works on social change. One of their more intriguing volumes is entitled, *The Human Meaning of Social Change*.[1] In the introduction are two interesting observations.

"It can plausibly be argued . . . that it will be more important in the future to understand [people's] images or psychological definitions of complex social situations than it may have been in the past."

". . . we are willing to imagine that the ultimate unit of meaning for all social structure, economic organization, technological development, and policy is the individual. . . ."

People are the measure of success, participation and social advancement. Whatever makes people more able to act, feel and be human with all the emotion, rationality and unpredictableness humanness entails—that becomes the measure of life. The magnitude of this admission is almost too great to comprehend! The vaunted scientific and technological thought patterns that have guided and compelled us as a society are now in a different context. Now, according to these authors, there is reason to believe that people and their feelings and thoughts should be given precedence over science and technology!

Social scientists are just reaching the point where local church people have been for years, the point of demanding that participation in organizations such as the church be on their terms rather than upon institutional terms. This means that the model of the church is one of owners-participants. Communication and accountability are being demanded. Only time and experience will show how well the church can respond and how willing those making the demands will be to assume a responsible place in the church.

Questions for Discussion

1. Do you refer to the church as "my"? What do you mean by it?
2. How can we get people to "own" programs and decisions in the church? Do you think doing so is important?
3. Have you observed any strain between leaders and followers in your church? How do you account for that?
4. Have you experienced oppression or paternalism in the church? Can you see how others might have?
5. What ways do you propose for your church to broaden its base of participation? Do you work hard at getting the inactive and disenchanted involved?
6. How do you find out about people's interest in tasks in the church? How do you get them involved after you discover their interests?
7. What is meant by "human" in the Christian context?

5 decisions

"We certainly appreciate you women coming out on a night like this to talk about the new minister. We will take these matters under consideration and let you know what we as a church council can do."

"When, did you say? Well, it probably won't be for another month or so at the earliest."

After the three women had left the room, the church council sat in silence for a couple of minutes. Then several propositions for action were offered, none of them very enthusiastically. Finally, the chairperson suggested that the matter be postponed until the next meeting. The members agreed and turned to other matters.

Sound familiar? It is the scene in church councils across the country. The room and issues change but the indecisiveness is common. Apparently, decisions can be made readily only when the issues are quite specific, for example, those concerned with details of finances. A part of the reason is that specifics can be made into a "yes-no" situation. More complex issues involving human relations cannot be so categorized and therefore tend to be avoided or postponed as long as possible.

Decision making is a difficult and trying experience for groups. Groups, especially those including persons with differing points of view, take much time before coming to a decision. They need to explore the issues in detail and develop a set of actions that are open to them as a group.

Issues that can be put in terms of yes-no dichotomies, such as establishing a time for a meeting, how much to pay a secretary and the like, may take time but decisions are made and actions taken. Deciding upon the group's position on issues involving people's convictions is a long and tiresome process. In fact, there is often a good chance that no decision will be made.

The influence of pluralism and sophistication in the use of organizational procedures complicates decision making. Those who have gone through the experience of making decisions in a church council that attempts to remain sensitive to the needs of various interest groups know that it becomes vexing. One person, tired of listening to such a debate recently, whispered:

"I wish those people would just go home and leave us alone so we could decide this thing!"

As a matter of fact, "those people" will not go home. Committed persons with varying backgrounds are asking to be heard by the church before programs are started and money spent. They will be around during debates and there when the votes are cast. They are determined to influence the vote because they feel that what the church does affects them. Thus, as pluralism increases, decisions of most types will not be easily arrived at and solutions to problems will be hard to agree upon.

Diversity means that more people will demand a greater voice in decisions, and as a result there will be no single decision but a series of decisions that result in programs. This happens now as local church committees decide upon their tasks, needs and programs. As a broader range of persons are involved in these committees the resulting decisions will represent a different perspective and interpretation of the life and work of the church.

These changes in perspective may prove difficult to accept by those who view the church as a tradition-maintaining institution. Conversely, the perspectives may not be changed enough for some who feel the church is too bound by institutional rigidity. Yet decisions will need to be made, with some being grounded in tradition and others being more prophetic, and the pluralistic mix will not always allow predictable results.

It is easy to see that the ability of a church council to handle conflict is and will become increasingly important in the church's decision making. Church leaders often feel guilty when conflict is generated or becomes a major part of the decision making process. Yet conflict is natural and is integral to decisions when diversity is a part of life. As diversity increases, the opportunity for conflict will also increase in the church.

Organizational adjustments in denominations and local churches have produced a lack of clarity as to who can and should make various kinds of decisions. Who plans and sets up the budget? Who determines how the building is to be used? Who sets up an experimental mission program in the community? Is it a matter for the Administrative Board or the Program Board? Answers to these and related questions have deep consequences for responsibility and accountability.

Also complicating decision making in the church is its unique character. People turn to the church in search of the elusive mystery of being. They feel that decisions from the church should somehow be more holy and deep than decisions from other organizations. Thus, decision making in the church is intertwined with theological and ethical imperatives. There is always a need for judgment and scriptural cross checking. The church must march to a tune different from that of other organizations, and as a consequence, decisions are often slow in coming.

These five factors influencing decision making indicate that in the future it will become more complex, more time consuming and probably more representative of the desires of its members. The type of leadership needed to help with the decision making processes will need to be articulate, sophisticated, sympathetic and patient. This kind of leadership, as suggested previously, will need to be found, trained and supported.

Leadership, however, is not the only key to decision making. The use of different models of decision making can help increase the effectiveness, lessen the conflict and deal with diverse representation. Four models can be used in the church at various times and on particular issues. These models can be adapted and varied as the need arises, or used in conjunction with one another.

1. Rules and Regulations Model

In this model, a person makes a motion, it gets a second, discussion takes place and a vote is made. The majority vote carries the day. This process is familiar and we have used it in the church over the years. While few persons are really expert in the details of this model, everyone who attends church meetings knows the rudiments of motion making, seconding, points of order, questions for information, calling the question and other essentials.

General familiarity is perhaps an overstatement. Rather, some people know how to make the process pay off for themselves and their causes. Minority groups, at the beginning of their rise into an effective force, found the going rough because opponents were skilled in making the process a roadblock to decisions. As one person said recently: "It is easy to control a group using this method because I know how. In fact, I think that I could control, with the help of a few others, the decisions of any large sized convention."

It is difficult to see, if this is true, how the majority can rule under this model. It is not difficult to understand that there is a winner and a loser—the group with the most persons in attendance who share its point of view will be the winner, and whoever opposes is the loser. This certainly does not mean

47

that the majority wins. It means that one person or group is able to get enough votes at the meeting to defeat an opponent. The implications should not be lost on the church.

In political situations, the model generates a "loyal opposition." The loser is supposed to become a protagonist to make sure that the interests supported by the minority are not neglected. Occasionally bipartisan support for a cause overcomes the loyal opposition theme. This is the theory and a good bit of the practice in politics.

In the church, the person either wins or loses. The loyal opposition concept does not apply because the church does not have that many rewards to give out. Thus a person either wins or leaves. On critical issues the rules and regulations model enforces alienation between the loser and the winner. While this alienation may be controlled and channeled, it is nevertheless a wedge that forces people apart over time.

Winners and losers establish their own sides. It is not necessary to document the effects of this in local churches, since nearly everyone has had the experience. The use of only a rules and regulations model will not provide continuing opportunity for dialogue between persons with opposing points of view even in the context of the church. Alternative models need to be used.

2. Consensus Model

The Quakers call this getting a "sense of the meeting." This model of decision making does not discount dissent, since it encourages all participants to express their points of view. It then calls for someone to attempt to gauge the feelings of the group so that a decision can be made that has the support of all or most of the group members.

This process takes a good deal of time and patience and has a set of rules which, for instance, govern the number of times a person may speak. It insists upon the expression of opinion from many or all of the people in the group. As a consequence, decisions are owned by most of the people, who are then willing to help implement them. The fact of conflict is very present and must be dealt with in the course of arriving at a consensus.

This model requires that respect for the viewpoint of others be maintained. The worth of an individual is maintained even though that person may disagree quite strongly with the majority. The model also allows for every person to "win" in the sense that action can be taken only after a consensus is reached. This obviously means that in some cases the only action possible is doing nothing.

48

The model can be best used in small groups and in situations where the issues are divisive and emotionally charged. It is more difficult for large groups such as congregational meetings. When used it is possible to conduct a series of "straw votes" to help pull the group toward consensus.

Straw votes test potential consensus on parts of the issue under discussion. When used repeatedly, the straw vote technique is helpful in maintaining a sense of perspective on an issue while moving the group toward a final decision.

3. Priority Model

A second alternative to the rules and regulations model is known as the priority or ranking model. It is the identification and listing of alternative actions and then rating these actions according to feasibility. A considerable amount of work before meetings must be done, to provide the information around which alternative courses of action can be developed.

This technique is often used in small groups such as church committees. It is especially helpful when a church is planning the next year's program.

When used in larger meetings such as congregational meetings, the congregation is divided into small groups, which work on different issues and then bring their alternatives to the larger group for final decisions. When there are several small groups working on many issues, the number of alternatives may be quite large. Experience has shown, however, that the number of practical alternatives is limited and more than one of the small groups will usually suggest essentially the same alternative.

The larger group then must work through the alternatives to arrive at the most feasible course of action. The working through process usually includes a listing of the assets and liabilities attached to each of the alternatives. Sometimes called "force-fielding," this technique puts down for the entire group's information the possible consequences of each alternative. This procedure allows the group to have a significant amount of responsibility for the future effects of their present decisions.

This model provides a maximum amount of participation by members of the larger group through their small group work. It respects the opinions of all persons as these come through the small groups in the form of alternative courses of action. It does not eliminate conflict but it does channel it constructively. It allows a person to compromise rather than be a total loser or a complete winner.

Indeed, there are few winners and losers in the sense described under the rules and regulations model. The ranking model is a process for reaching realistic compromises in group settings. It deals with information and feelings in such a way that the large group can feel that ownership rests with the congregation and not with a pastor or two or three members. At the same time, this process takes time and is best done in two-day meetings. When critical issues are being discussed it is usually in the best interests of the group to take the time away from its normal setting to work out its priority decisions.

A local church found that when it took time to get away from the church its planning work got done; when it stayed in the church, its work did not get finished. It looked into the reasons for this. It found that people who went away focused their attention upon the topics at hand and did not leave to go home for quick errands. The atmosphere of the surroundings seemed to be a stimulant. The fact of working on a clearly defined task helped people do the task.

4. Negotiation Model

Negotiation is a part of every decision in the church. The negotiation decision making model is one in which a series of committees or subgroups make tentative decisions and then negotiate or compromise those decisions in ever-increasing and larger groups until the entire church has made a common decision. This has been used in some churches in the process of budget building through committees, as well as to determine the types of social witness activities in which a church should be engaged.

Some church people criticize the results of this model because they look like watery gruel. True, there is a chance that the lowest common denominator will be developed for programs. Yet even this will be a stronger basis of corporate action than the results of a few pushing their wills upon the many through a manipulation of the rules and regulations model.

The negotiation model requires that each group know its own mind about the issues under discussion. It also requires that the groups become competing entities with other groups in the church. Neither of these situations is detrimental in itself but they must be seen in the context of the church's larger purposes and handled with skilled and committed leadership to accomplish the desired end of ownership and participation.

In this model, a mix of the membership of the entire church is essential. This mix can be developed in the subgroup process and participate freely in the negotiations. A deliberate effort to create and use diversity will generate conflict but, in the small group settings, this can be handled more easily than in other types of settings.

Each of these three alternative models—consensus, priority, and negotiation—has proved useful in local churches, and should be used increasingly. These models can be used with few people (as long as groups contain 2 or 3 persons each) or with many (the maximum for effective small groups is 12 to 15 participants). In many ways they are less prone to manipulation by articulate and powerful persons in the congregation. They do require skilled leadership, but this can be developed if necessary.

Nature of a Decision

Whatever model is used, however, the important thing for a church is the decision. A decision signifies that a group has taken a plunge into the unknown. A decision separates the *possibility* of doing something from the *actuality* of doing something. It is a separation of the ought from the because, the might be from the is. It is an awakening from dream to action.

This movement into purposive activity follows a process of selecting among alternative courses of actions. A church, because of its unique calling and purpose, needs to make these choices in a deliberate fashion and at a pace slower than many groups are willing to function. However, some churches act on a "crisis" decision making psychology. Simply stated, this means that everything they face is in a state of crisis. While there are emergencies that need immediate attention, however, most decisions facing a church can be made over a period of time rather than in the haste of a single meeting.

Few human situations are new, and even crisis situations have a history. A few years ago, national church bodies developed a program called the "Crisis in the Nation," an effort to deal with the tense urban situations especially as these fanned the flames between whites and blacks. Except for the rhetoric (and even this might have been used before), there was nothing new in the urban situations, but the new program provided a platform upon which some people could speak. The decisions that emanated from the program were generally ineffectively implemented and poorly timed. It was conceived and put into motion with a crisis mentality.

If a church desires to make an impact upon a situation and to really implement its decision, it will take enough time to let its members work through alternatives before making a decision. This is the reason for suggesting that churches use

51

more than one means for making decisions. For once the decision is made with the church members owning it, it becomes possible for the church to put its resources behind it. Hasty decisions run out of steam before long because people are not committed to them.

Decisions involve personal and institutional directions and needs. They include staff persons and members in their consequences. The decision to relocate a church, for example, can be made by a relatively few people—but it has been known to rip a church apart. The decision may reflect certain institutional needs of some groups in the church, especially as these relate to a change in residence, and some personal needs of some leaders. It may be based upon urban deterioration. However, the decision cannot be made with only a few interests represented when in the long run it affects many institutions and people who are not part of the decision.

This points up the second aspect of a decision. It lets the world know how certain people feel about an issue. This is really a part of the life of the church. It has a mission about which it must speak. Its decisions need to reflect its witness to the gospel of Christ. The church cannot just let decisions happen because it needs to take a stand.

The mystery of the gospel provides a base as well as a sense of purpose and identity for the church as it takes a stand. When the church speaks from the basis of the gospel on social issues, personal ethics, justice and salvation, it speaks with a clear and honorable history. When the church fails to speak specifically to the issues of its situation, when it fails to recognize and go on record against cheating and stealing of any form, when it does not speak out against injustice, the church is making decisions of inaction that are not in keeping with its purpose.

Perhaps it is this need to take a stand that makes church groups sometimes hesitant to decide. It is easier to drift into a decision than it is to make one. When a group drifts, it can eventually get off the hook by saying that events shaped the situation so that they had no control over the final decision. This is a clever and sophisticated way out of being identified as having taken a stand for God.

A group with a sense of its own identity and purpose makes decisions that reflect its identity and purpose, in spite of situations. When the church does not know what it is about, it can be carried to and fro by the tides of circumstance.

The third aspect of a decision is that action must follow. A decision is made so that something can get done, not just to have something on paper. The assumption is that people who are committed and have something specific to do can and will want to act. Indeed, they will act responsibly. The key words are commitment and specificity.

The three alternatives to the rules and regulations model are means for ensuring both commitment and specificity. When church groups can begin to use these techniques in a way that guarantees the integrity, worth and opinions of each member, it is quite likely that decision making will improve considerably. Not only decision making will improve but responsible action will become a frequent and visible result of decisions.

Questions for Discussion

1. What are some factors in your church that affect decision making?
2. How do your church groups handle the more complex decisions regarding human needs? When does conflict arise?
3. Which of the four models of decision making does your church use most often? How can you best use the other models?
4. Does your church take stands for or against issues based upon its Christian purpose? How does, or can, it develop a process to ensure participation and the opportunity for people to dissent?
5. What decisions are needed by your church now to make it more alive and creative? How can you help get those decisions made?

6 conflict

The Scripture says, "Where two or three are gathered, I will be there." (Matthew 18:20) The gospel message places God in the midst of the human situation. This is critical to remember because it is an axiom of human groups that where two or three are gathered, disputes and conflict will arise. Conflict is a normal and natural result of human interaction. People are not alike; they do not think or feel alike and should not be expected always to get along. There is nothing subversive or dangerous about conflict. The problem with conflict is not so much that it interrupts social relations in organizations, but that conflicts are put aside, ignored or blown completely out of proportion or context. In the midst of these tendencies, however, there is the promise of redemptive love.

Because of the feeling that the church should be a place where love is expressed and forgiveness is a part of life, conflict situations are glossed over or become so threatening that they cannot be dealt with constructively. Since conflict is a common part of human life, it should be possible for the church to deal creatively with it, not to shrink from it or to approach it with fear and suspicion. Jesus was a master at handling conflict. He changed from absorbing ridicule to confronting money changers in the Temple. He demonstrated that conflict is not always handled by turning the other cheek or maintaining a loving attitude. His example suggests that the church needs to change its attitude about conflict, recognize its worth and devise means for working through it to more firm and healthy relationships.

The word conflict brings to mind an image of people in some sort of physical confrontation. Seldom, however, does conflict in the church mean that persons are engaged in physical combat. Rather, it means words and noncombatant action. This can be very dangerous, because people battling with words maneuver themselves into ideological positions that may not represent their true feelings. Once an ideological position is taken, it cannot be changed during the conflict except at the risk of loss of status, or "face." No one is quite strong enough by himself to accept such loss; we tend, therefore, not to change our position.

In the church, the opportunity exists for allowing people to change. In fact, this is the impact of the gospel. The ability of the church to provide personal protection and maintain personal worth during conflict is a test of its adherence to the gospel. The loving community does not avoid conflict but it does help people not to lose sight of the end goal of common worship and witness to the Lord through Christ.

Conflict is not to be taken lightly, but it must not be considered or allowed to become a detriment or threat to persons. It is an important human process during which a person may test his or her own position and identity with others. Conflict, viewed in this manner, is interaction around issues and ideas. It contains the potential for growth and creativity, which can be fulfilled only when people feel that they are in a supportive context. The people involved and those observing, in order to be supportive, must respect the integrity of the disputants and be committed to helping them either resolve their dispute or find a basis for common action on other issues.

The thesis of this chapter is that the church can and should provide a supportive context for creative conflict. This statement is based on a healthy respect for the place of conflict in the development and enhancement of human experience. The following thoughts may provide some alternatives to the paralysis that often accompanies conflict in the church.

Conflict, Trust and Respect

The most important point about conflict is that disputes do not need to become hindrances to cooperation and respect. It might be nice to live in a social situation in which there was no conflict, and cooperation and respect were common ingredients of life. On the other hand, such an existence might be dull and unexciting. It was not the existence of any biblical setting. In fact, it is in conflict that most creativity can occur. If no one ever has an idea that causes discomfort or challenges the ideas or behaviors of others, there is little or no opportunity for innovation. The prophets are examples of challenges that created new ways or opportunities for dealing with life.

This is not to advocate initiating conflict with some long-shot hope that creativity may be a result. Quite enough conflict is generated just by living together. On the other hand, it is helpful at times to play the adversary to ideas or habits of acting, and help groups gain new insights. It is difficult to come up with answers to problems until someone identifies the problems and asks the questions. Until the issue of the roles of women in the church was raised, for example, most church people ignored it or let others deal with it. Once the issue was raised, programs, conversations and conflict were generated. The result is that it has begun to get attention and some creative solutions may begin to emerge.

Having said this, however, we must acknowledge the difficulty of developing a personal sense of cooperation with persons or groups with whom we disagree or feel uncomfortable. When a person is put into an uncomfortable and hostile environment it is possible to be civil and talk, but a minimum of real communication takes place. There is little sharing of real feeling or insights about anything of significance. In short, a person is generally unwilling to trust another in combat even though only words are used.

Yet it is possible to achieve deeper communication and sharing by seeking out areas of commonality for the combatants. This means finding a common issue, experience or concern on which persons might be willing to talk openly with each other.

Politics is taboo for some people because they know that if they did begin a discussion, conflict would damage their relationship. These same persons talk with and enjoy each other when politics are not a part of the conversation. Could not this technique of avoiding or limiting discussion on issues that engender unchanging positions be used in church settings?

The most obvious answer is yes. The problem is, how? Three quick ideas might be thrown out for consideration. One is to separate the emotional overtones from the objective and factual issues of the case. In this way, a person does not continually have to fight on the basis of feelings. When this separation is possible, conflict can be worked at more systematically and constructively.

A second idea is to separate the disagreement into parts or segments. This creates an opportunity to deal with discrete pieces of issues that do not produce conflict. Most issues can be broken into several parts, and each part can be dealt with separately. It is important, once the pieces have been identified, to begin with the less sensitive ones and work these out before getting on to the very sensitive issues. This procedure develops a degree of trust between people and builds integrity into the solution. It also provides people an opportunity to build bridges of communication, which will be helpful as they seek solutions to the more emotionally charged parts of the conflict.

A third method is to back away from the situation and issues so that a new perspective can be given to the reasons for the conflict. This is known as a "cooling-off" period. During such a time, each person can work on possible solutions independently of the others. These possible solutions are then tested.

Many conflicts in the church could produce creative results instead of divisive problems if these simple techniques were implemented. Most of us use them daily at work or in the family. Why not give them a try in the church?

The use of any or all of these techniques during church conflicts allows the persons or groups involved to maintain trust and respect for each other. This is not to suggest that trust and respect are felt at all times during the conflict. Indeed, trust and respect must be earned. None of us is going to trust or respect another person just because we know it is the right thing to do. As Christians we can, and do, attempt to maintain these feelings but as sinners we often fail. That is why forgiveness is such an important part of the church.

Trust comes with sharing difficulties, being aware of each other's strength and weaknesses, and feeling that others are seeking to find mutually acceptable ways of working through those difficulties. Trust is an attitude that develops because a person is willing to risk a part of him or herself in dealing with others. This risk is taken because one person is convinced that the other person is functioning out of his or her integrity.

Trust is the cornerstone of respect. It is impossible to trust someone without having respect for that person and his or her integrity. Perhaps the respect is limited to certain parts of the person's behavior. In fact, we only deal with those parts of another person's life that touch upon us in one way or another. We do not generally deal with a whole person even in the church.

Consider, for example, the testimonials gathered by the press about persons who have committed acts that astonish friends and neighbors, like multiple murders. The general public is shocked to hear of the respect held for the murderers by friends and associates. In fact, there should be no shock because the friends and associates limit their respect to the behavior they know. Thus, the integrity of the person from their point of view is based upon what they can observe.

We know that we need to feel and exhibit trust and respect for others. We should be equally aware that the other person or groups with which we deal are in the same position. They have to trust us! How strange that seems, that someone would even question our motives or good intentions. Yet others have the same feelings of uncertainty and apprehension about us that we have about them. It is for this reason that risks in relationships must be undertaken. In fact, every relationship, in the church or out, is a risk on the part of all parties concerned.

The fact that all relationships are adventures in risk should provide some clues about dealing with conflict. If conflict is approached with an effort at respect and a desire to build cooperation, chances are it can be worked through, and the dangerous schisms and splits of groups so common in the church can be minimized and circumscribed. On the other hand, when a person or group approaches a conflict with no feeling of hope, trust, respect or idea that cooperation can be achieved on even small parts of a common task, resolution is impossible.

In general, resolution depends upon the desire of participants to arrive at a solution. The risk involved is not really of oneself so much as a risk for the sake of a common good. A counselor often tells one partner in a marriage to risk himself or herself a bit more through sharing ideas and hopes so that new grounds for respect can be opened up. This type of risk may not pay off, but it is the best hope for the beginning of resolution.

Conflict and Supportive Relationships

Personal and organizational growth takes place when there is a supportive and accepting atmosphere, not when antagonistic attitudes are prevalent. This is a "common sense" philosophy most of us know intuitively but it is often overlooked in the heat of living. It is this philosophy which undergirds the popular transactional approach to life suggested in the book, *I'm O.K.—You're O.K.*[1]

Growth takes place as one successfully confronts and overcomes obstacles. Part of successful growth is a person's ability to deal with pressures and defeats. However, this ability is developed in social situations and depends a great deal upon the kind of emotional support given by others during times of conflict and crisis. John Donne expressed this in "No Man Is an Island." We are dependent upon each other and our outlooks are fashioned by the kinds of support and assistance we receive from others.

At first glance, the church should be the place where such support is the rule and not the exception, or at least a norm toward which all church people strive. However, we live in an imperfect world and must work through all kinds of personal problems at the same time as we take on issues and concerns raised by others. In such situations it is often difficult if not impossible to be kind and supportive of those who initiate or prolong conflict and disagreement. We must recognize that "We know better than we do."

This is not an attempt to excuse our inability to be supportive most of the time. We know our imperfection. We know that when there is a threat to our status and position, we are not going to be supportive. On the other hand, most times we could benefit from change even though it looks like a threat. Acceptance of change is a matter of taking a long rather than a short view. If we could think about eventualities rather than maintenance of our present situation, most conflicts would be less severe.

Conflict, to be most creative, must be placed in the context of supportive relationships. These do not necessarily exist naturally but, in the Christian community, need to be created. Such creation is possible a good many times only when a person is willing to risk him or herself, which requires a good bit of rethinking of our own values and needs. Most of us have worked too hard to assure ourselves of our own identity and place in life to put it on the line in a conflict situation in the church. Yet that is exactly what has to be done if we are to deal collectively with issues that divide and separate us. At such times, collective examination of our expectations of the church, our beliefs and our norms is in order.

No one of us has a corner on all the truth. Most of us have a little of it, but there is so much that we do not have that what we can claim is very tiny. Yet, we feel that we do have the truth and we attempt to, indeed must, protect it. We seldom recognize that others also have truth from which we could benefit by sharing. In our more rational moments, we know that sharing becomes possible only when mutual supportive relationships are established. Maintaining those relationships, extremely difficult as it is, provides an alternative to suspicion and fear, which conflict tends to generate.

Tensions between persons and groups in the church are to be expected, and working through them can become creative. It can become creative when we have the grace and desire to look beyond our own side of an issue to see the validity of other positions. Then the hard step comes. In conjunction with people holding other points of view, recognizing that God's love and Jesus' example applies to both them and us, we must attempt to develop some common understandings and actions. When we are unable to see beyond ourselves and develop a narrowness of spirit, churches split, ministers and laity separate, and persons develop untenable positions on issues facing churches—even small issues. The church needs to use some of the simple techniques that have proved valuable in labor negotiations, sports and other forms of structured human activity.

People use several methods for handling conflict in their nonchurch environments, and we will look at four of them here: (1) withdrawing from conflict; (2) finding a nonthreatening environment in which to discuss differences; (3) attempting to restate the issues in order to reduce the amount of emotion laden language; and (4) using a third party as a negotiator. Each of these is a creative strategy when used at the appropriate time.

Withdrawal from Conflict

The easiest way to handle conflict, at least in the short range, is to withdraw from it. This is simply done most of the time. It is a matter of refusing to talk any longer. It may also take the form, as sometimes happens in domestic confrontations, of one party leaving the house or the scene of the dispute.

The result of withdrawal is that conflict ceases because one of the participants has chosen not to take any further risks. This, while not necessarily a good strategy at all times, may be highly effective in certain situations. The problem occurs in attempting to determine when and where to use such a strategy. While there are no fool-proof formulas for determining the appropriate time for withdrawal, some general observations may be helpful.

Withdrawal is a good strategy when conflict has reached the point where it is impossible to separate emotion from reason, fact from assumption and issue from personality. As noted earlier, an important step in conflict resolution is separating emotion from fact. In some cases, such as in deciding to relocate a church, replace a minister, or discussions of theology, persons begin to choose irrational positions and defend them to the point where reason cannot intrude on their senses.

It takes only a little sensitivity on the part of those in a dispute to know when emotion has overcome all possibility for establishing reason as a basis for discussion. When this does become apparent, it is wise to stop the discussion and withdraw from the conflict scene. This physical withdrawal will help the parties compose themselves. Physical withdrawal and reentry will not, however, guarantee a rational discussion at the next session.

Withdrawal is also a good strategy when a proposal that begins to make sense is submitted by one of the parties. It is a good idea to remove oneself from a situation of some heat to a place where there is some degree of calm and rationality.

This can do two things. In the first place, it can help provide a "safe" place for initial reactions and then a situation in which analysis of the proposal may occur. In the second place, withdrawal for study provides the possibility of developing a rational counterproposal. This is the benefit of "cooling off" periods, which can aid immeasurably in the process of conflict resolution.

Withdrawal for either of these two reasons does not mean that constructive work at resolving the conflict cannot continue. Efforts should continue, even if the parties just write down their thoughts and the opposing positions. This exercise at least visualizes positions and thus helps make them more objective and less open to emotional coloring.

But withdrawal is not always a creative technique. It is not good, for example, when the problem has not been clearly identified. There must be some reason for the outbursts, accusations or anger generated during conflict, and to withdraw before some of the sources are identified is to prolong the conflict because only emotions are involved. It makes the beginnings of conflict resolution impossible because there is nothing to resolve other than the fact that two or more persons are not getting along.

It is also inappropriate to withdraw when one party is attempting to clarify his own and the other person's position. When this begins to occur, the process of conflict resolution has begun. Staying in the conflict at such a point is often painful, because it means that the underlying causes of conflict must be surfaced for all the world to see. It also frequently means that one's own position will not be as valid as supposed, so one or both parties are now open to the loss of status or face.

This should not really be the case. Everyone knows that overstatement and extreme positions are the rule rather than the exception during a conflict. This is to be expected, and to accept it is to admit our humanity, as well as to display some Christian underpinning. It is also to begin to set the stage for trust development by showing our desire to work together in addressing the need to resolve the situation.

The first step in conflict resolution is admission of positions that need to be modified. This is not necessarily a formal admission and may be made only after a good deal of coaxing. It is essential, however, before the next step—developing alternatives for resolving conflict—can be considered. One must agree that his or her position needs to be changed before he or she is willing to discuss what those changes ought to be and how they are to be implemented. Even then, conflict resolution is a matter of conjecture but at least it is more nearly possible than when people are totally and publicly convinced that they are right and the other side is wrong.

Withdrawal can be employed with good results only at certain times. Most of us employ it when it is painful to continue in the conflict process. But pain is not necessarily a good reason, for it may be a sign that a group has reached the point of healing. About the only realistic guideline is the suggestion that withdrawal be used as a last resort. The techniques of separating emotion from fact, keeping quiet for a short time to "cool off" a bit and attempting to break the disagreement into parts on which some negotiation can take place should all be attempted first. It is important to let the Spirit work also by providing some openness through prayer. When these do not bring a new perspective, break off the dispute and try another approach to handling the conflict.

Neutral Ground

An alternative to withdrawal is to find neutral ground for continuing the discussions. People can usually be persuaded to talk over differences of opinion even about sensitive issues in a nonthreatening environment. One of the most successful tactics of a major ecumenical organization is to bring together leaders of various denominations and allow them to talk together about issues in a setting away from their home territories. Away from home people can deal more freely with topics that would cause only animosity in their more familiar surroundings. It is not that the issues or the people have changed, but since they do not have to play to any of their "home-town audiences," they are freed from certain expectations about their roles and behaviors.

Finding neutral ground is one of the bases for legal systems, which have combatants appear in a court setting to solve their cases. The court is a place of neutrality and allows for a rational discussion of issues in a dispute.

When people are forced to take a side in the presence of friends as well as foes, the conflict changes from a disagreement to an ideological issue, which can splinter churches and create life-long enemies. If the church is to be a healing and reconciling institution, it ought to learn that conflict may be redirected into constructive channels by allowing participants to move to other physical environments or at least change the setting so that the people in the dispute do not have to play to their audiences.

Even when movement to another physical setting is impossible, it may help to separate the disputants from other persons. Let them go at it in private. Let another person act as reconciliator. It is much easier to change positions or to grow calm when there is no audience. Providing a "battling room" is a technique that can assist churches to move beyond conflict and into some creative solutions to issues which need attention but generate tensions.

Restating the Issue

Another relatively simply alternative to withdrawal is to restate an issue, changing it from a personalized attack upon a person or an office to an issue that can be addressed with reason and some calm. This restatement process is an effort to make the various elements of a dispute objective so that several parties can react to those elements rather than to each other.

In a recent meeting of ministers and laity, a statement made by a young minister was considered by older ministers to be an attack upon them. The young man said that these other ministers got in the way of new young pastors. Since the participants in the discussion were highly identified with each side of the issue, it was appropriate to restate the issue along nonemotional lines.

This may seem to be skirting the issue. However, to have discussed the emotionally charged statement of the young minister would have created only hostility, which could be surfaced and dealt with in a more creative fashion in another setting and at another time. In the interest of accomplishing the goals set before the group at that time, it was necessary to redirect the focus of the conflict so that the group could deal with it objectively.

This is certainly not a revolutionary way of handling conflict. It does suggest that someone in a group in which conflict is imminent can take the lead in restating the issue so that emotion and fact are separated and the real issue can be dealt with. In such restatement, the process of healing can begin.

Third Party

There is another way to handle conflict in the church: engage a third party who can help groups work through the conflict and the issues that created it. This is a strategy used in labor disputes, when arbitrators are engaged to help union and management reach settlements.

Even when there is much evidence that a third party can be useful in cases of conflict, the church often does not use such counsel. Perhaps conflict is so threatening to members that they cannot acknowledge its presence in the church. Theology does say love your enemies, and some church people feel that it is a sin even to recognize that such benevolent feelings do not always stir their hearts and those of others.

It usually takes some type of conflict, however, to clarify who or what the enemies are, either in the church or outside it. When conflict is suppressed, enemies become covertly identified, and persons who have feelings of antagonism toward them feel guilty for violating the theology of love.

This roundabout sense of sin does not recognize reality. People live in social situations that by definition are conflict producing and competitive. It is unreasonable to believe that the church is not a scene for conflict and competition. The conflict may be a result of people's vying for leadership positions, status or some special reward and not liking to lose. This causes a simple case of conflict. It may be necessary even then, however, to use a third party.

The point is that it is important and necessary to have an impartial third party help find ways and means to reach compromise positions to maintain the status and integrity of each party while they come to a settlement. It is much healthier and more in keeping with the ethic of forgiveness to have a third party alleviate conflict between two segments of a church than to have the conflict result in two new churches. It is much more productive, for example, for the church to have a choir than to dissolve it because of the conflict between it and the pastor.

The characteristics needed by the third party are tolerance, patience, humor and respect for each of the participants. These are the qualities of a good number of church people, and it is probable that in any dispute or conflict an effective third party can be found within the church. The point is that such a person *should be found*. Dependence upon the pastor to perform the third party role should be diminished, for he is often one of the participants in the conflict.

One final note: it is sometimes possible to eliminate conflict by being careful of what we say and how we say it. How many times have we wished that we had not said something because it only leads to trouble! How many times have we wished that we had thought before we spoke! The message is quite clear— do take the time to think before speaking. Think not only about immediate effects but long term repercussions of what we say.

The phrasing of our statements could also be improved in many cases so that they could lead to fruitful rather than disputative discussions. Since conflict usually draws upon the irrational and emotional parts of people, it is best not to use words as red flags. For instance, many people cannot discuss the issue of racism without conflict because the word itself is pejorative. It is like hitting them with a club or waving a dirty picture in front of them. It is possible, however, to talk rationally about some of the problems of discrimination faced by various minority groups and the probable causes for that discrimination. It is also possible to probe why one holds particular attitudes and try to isolate the antecedents to such attitudes.

This approach may be much too tame for some reformers or change agents who are much more psychologically oriented to continuous conflict. As fate would have it, most people are not so geared. They would rather not deal with conflict or conflict situations. Therefore, it becomes necessary to work at their level rather than begin at a different and quite jarring level of conflict. It will be difficult enough to work through conflict situations without continually stirring up the situation.

Conflict Resolution

To summarize, the first and most important step in conflict resolution is to agree upon the problem, for no problem will ever be solved if people do not talk to the same issue. Not only must they talk to the same issue but they must also be able to see it apart from all other issues. This means that the focus on the problem must be exaggerated at the outset so that a common understanding of the dimensions of the problem can be developed.

The second step is to separate it into several parts, which may also be segregated on a scale that moves from the least to the most sensitive aspects of the problem.

The third step is to take each part of the problem and work with it until a mutual agreement is reached. This piece by piece development of solutions should never be done outside the context of the total problem. It may be possible to use, according to the part of the problem being dealt with, the various techniques for handling conflict including finding neutral ground, restating issues and involving a third party to help with the negotiations.

The fourth step, after a total set of agreements has been established, is to publicly affirm the resolution of conflict. This may be as simple as saying that "we have resolved our differences." No matter the form, the public statement establishes the good faith of each party and the mutuality of the agreement before audiences. This is very important, because audiences can then begin to enforce the agreement through social pressure.

A fifth step is to have someone neutral designated to help "keep the peace." This is quite important. Such a person becomes a formal communication link between the two parties and can help nip in the bud potential conflict situations. Such a person must be trusted by all parties.

These five steps may seem overly elaborate to some church people. They really are not. We use them every day in dealing with each other. We find that one part of the process may need to be elaborated while another can be skimped a bit. However, conflict resolution must be accomplished, at least in social groups, in a rationalized manner. The above process has often been used, and it works!

Questions for Discussion

1. How do we react to and deal with conflict?
2. Do we have a technique to deal with conflict? What are the major parts of the technique?
3. How can we be supportive of a person or group with whom we disagree?
4. If we withdraw from conflict, do we use the time to help think through our position?
5. What kinds of issues can we compromise on?
6. Do we use a third party often? When should we consider it?

7 practicalism and theology

Some people have almost a phobia about change. They need to get in on new activities, crazes and ideas all the time. They want to change as an end in itself. They become frustrated and bored if change is interrupted or slowed down. These people get new clothes, appliances, autos not because they are needed but because the new represents change.

There are others, however, who do not want anything changed. They are like the villagers in *Fiddler on the Roof*, existing because of tradition. They cannot explain why they do things as they do but, whatever the reasons, are unwilling to make any changes.

Most people are somewhere between these extremes. They are willing to change what they are doing or the way they are acting if and when someone can show to their satisfaction that a new way is more helpful for them. They change out of choice sometimes and at other times because they are forced by circumstances. For example, if new autos are equipped with new buzzer systems, people grow to accept them and expect them to perform as warning signals that seat belts are loose or that headlights have not been turned off.

People change because it is practical or in their self-interest. Even then, any given change covers only a small part of their lives or is introduced a little at a time into their experience. In many cases change is so gradual that it is unnoticed. Perhaps that is why parents with young people in college or away from home for the first time become a bit more tolerant or change oriented than they were previously. They have been gradually changing their outlook on life and have also changed expectations regarding their children. Perhaps this need for gradualism in change is the reason that churches that introduce too much change too quickly undergo crises of identification and purpose.

Indeed, any time one attempts to make something over or to implement a new way of doing a job, resistance must be expected. People are creatures of habit. Culture is built around habit and common expectations. Habit relieves us of the necessity to provide reasons for the way we do things. Thus, when a child continually poses the question, "Why?"

to his or her parents they lose composure. "That's just the way it is," is true. The reasons have long been forgotten.

While such a response is not always adequate for young people, it provides a sense of security and continuity to the answerer. Habit and *status quo* are generally comfortable, but it is uncomfortable to move out into new and strange ways of dress and behavior or to develop new attitudes. It is hard to change.

Change Is the Game

Change is the game we play when we attempt to get things done. There is no way that working in the world or church will not involve change. The degree of change we will face will depend partly upon our inclination to change but also upon the flexibility of the situation. The opportunity for conflict and creativity will always be present, and along with them, the potential for change.

This does not suggest that change is always positive. In fact, one who suggests change for change's sake may really be an advocate of the devil rather than a prophet of the future. Change (for a group) must always serve a larger purpose than to satisfy one person's needs and ego. Traditions are important, even though they may need to assume new meanings with each generation.

The determination of what change is beneficial in a group or an organization must always be made by a few people. This does not mean that small groups of people have it within their power to implement change or to demand that all others willingly accept the change. Far from it. Yet, change is made possible by the initiative of a few people of like mind. They keep pestering, talking and acting until someone else is concerned enough to change. In organizations it is inevitable that when change is suggested and supported by influential persons, the *status quo* will be inched one way or the other.

A person's attitude toward change will determine which side of the change game he or she will play, change or resist. In the end, there are no bystanders.

Church people are active and not passive! They need to do things about life and its problems. They, and therefore their churches, are activity oriented. A quick glance at any church calendar reveals a set of activities by the week or the month; some of them are age-grouped or sex-grouped and others "for the whole family." It seems that planners are afraid to let some free days creep into the church calendar.

One of the traits of a good pastor is that he is out getting people to join this or that group so that they will become "involved" in the church. This is certainly to be commended. People who take an interest in an organization get themselves involved by doing things such as leading an organization, becoming an officer in an auxiliary or the like.

Many times, however, in the midst of activity, not much of significance seems to be taking place. In fact, the church is like a giant sponge. It absorbs the activity of many people with little visible result to the community or nonmember. It grows internally but does not have the dynamism of a living organism. Thus it was that a great deal of questioning was raised during the late 1950's and the 1960's about the validity of the church with all of its business. It was criticized as culture bound, secular and irrelevant to people. All of its internal activity evidently was not being used effectively or efficiently to accomplish what some people thought the church should be doing.

The mood that developed in the church during the middle and late 1960's was one of getting involved in community action and social intervention. The comment of a Catholic bishop sums up the attitudes of many clergy and laity during these times. "The Church must get its shoes dirty. It has to help people!" These were good sentiments, and many in the church went out and got their shoes dirty. They marched and protested and stayed in jails. They were doing something about the social problems of their generation.

It will not take accumulated decades of perspective to realize that much good was accomplished by the "dirty feet" emphasis. On the other hand, this emphasis too must pass. It had its moment in the sun. It was born of a need to be free, and it must die as it becomes a limiting and restrictive way of meeting men's needs in new situations. Thus, the techniques and emphases for activities in the church must have life spans of varying lengths. Yet the need to continually develop and use new techniques or emphases to get something done about human conditions does not pass for church people. They will continue to experiment and prod to find new ways of dealing with new situations and old human predicaments like pride, intolerance, greed and unbelief.

Getting Things Done

Since church people are activity prone, it would be helpful to provide them with some handles to make their activity do the tasks of the church. These handles include a recognition that the way a person views an organization will have a great deal to do with how he or she becomes involved in it. It is also important to deal with short-range projects or activities as pieces of long-range goals. Another aspect of getting things done in the church is to provide a time table for involvement which makes sense to members. Each of these handles needs a bit more examination to become useful.

It is clear that people who feel comfortable in an organization will feel that they are doing things both for themselves and for others. It is equally clear that people who feel uncomfortable will not stay around long. Church leaders, faced with these facts, often ask, "Why?" They are constantly seeking out people's motives with the hope that if they can just find the right "turn-on" button, the church will be filled every week. A recent study showed that motives are the hopes and expectations of people translated into a reality by the social situation in which they live, work and worship.[1] Motives are really the possibilities of acting out hopes, which are either generated inside a person or imposed by the group to which a person belongs.

When faced with the church as an institution that can be used to get things done, people view it in three rather distinct ways. One way is to see it as an organization that is constrictive, restrictive and generally uncomfortable. They see it as providing form and structure to activity but not necessarily allowing for the normal human tendency to be individual. There are creeds and rules to inhibit behavior and outlaw pleasure. There are church leaders whose apparent task is to produce guilt for the smallest infraction of the most minute law of the organization.

An organization in this image is like a form-fitted garment with no allowance for extra bulges—it makes a person irritable and hard to get along with. In time, the organization becomes meaningful only in terms of its form and structure. This is quite apparent in some denominations that describe how local churches are to be organized. There are a certain number of officers and a series of contact persons with whom denominational officials can be in touch for special mailings and programs. There is a mission secretary, a worship chairperson, a series of educational contacts and keepers of finances. Then there are trustees and official governing bodies. All of these have quite specific functions and carefully defined duties.

This image of the instutution of the church gives one the impression of a gigantic mechanical monster, feeding on people's energies and skills. It robs them of time with their families; it takes an interest in doing things for the church and puts it to use in programs that are less than helpful and keeps it there by virtue of insinuated guilt; or it increases the importance of insignificant tasks so that the person in charge gets a distorted image of his own importance.

This view of a church is not very attractive to many people. It reeks of age and dust, or of a highly oiled and manipulated machine. It does not suggest an organization of humans working together on the problems of people.

A reaction to this view of organization is the image of any organization as unnecessary, to be avoided at any cost. A group of "free spirits" get together around certain issues of social importance and say they should act this way if things are to get accomplished. Each one pitches in and away they go.

The innovative ministries of the last decade are illustrations of such groups. History has shown that any group that continued without organization ended in oblivion. While it is important to be free of the stifling effects of form and structure, it is equally important to organize energies and people. Even creeds are needed so that a common framework of theology or philosophy can be developed and used as a reference point through time.

There is a third view of organization that can stand the test of time. It appears that every generation must go through the first two views before it can "discover" the third—that an organization can exist to channel and direct common energies to accomplish specific tasks. This is a logical and simple view of organizations. Perhaps because of its very logic and simplicity, people take a long time to come to this conclusion.

Institutions and organizations are to be used for getting things done; they are not entities created and ordained by God. No structure has been ordained as sacred and unbendable. Organizations are the creatures of people who share social experience. The most lasting of human organizations, including the family and the church, have been adapted and bent to fit the needs of the groups using the structures in varying situations. In this sense, the best structures are those that identify a set of needs and then help people select the roles they can play in meeting those needs.

This may sound chaotic but it really is not. As a young pastor who serves a small church can verify, members often accept titles just because they are asked. The pastor also knows that the essential work gets done not because of the titles but because people who are interested set about organizing themselves to do certain tasks. They may not be as particular about the definitions of their tasks as the pastor would like, but things do get done.

When this freedom to use the structure to meet needs is not

allowable, there develops a great deal of frustration within the organization, which in our time has often come out under the label of "anti-institutionalism." This is really a name given to the feeling that the structure is too tight for people to get involved in and find some fulfillment in their activity.

In a very practical vein, would it not be more humane to use the form and structure of the church to direct people's energies rather than fill organizational slots with names? The answer may be yes, but there are few pastors or denominational leaders willing to allow such freedom. They seem to fear that freedom will impede getting things done in the name of the church. No data exist to support such a fear; in fact, the opposite is true. Freedom within a framework of organization allows things to get done better and faster.

It would seem that the church organization should be used to stimulate and develop the creativity of people, in worship, education, social action or evangelism. Yet creativity must always be seen as an attempt to interpret the meaning of life through the form and structure of the church. It has continuity with the past and is always under the judgment, as well as the inspiration, of the Holy Spirit.

The activity proneness of church people can be channeled through the church to get things done in meaningful fashion. First, it is necessary to help develop the church in such a way that people no longer view it as a very tight and uncomfortable structure stifling individuals. A second task is to help people understand that the church needs form and organization, so that it can organize the common efforts of people and be effective. Finally, the view of the church as a stimulator and developer of people needs to be cultivated.

This latter view is seldom lasting. People are creatures of habit, and it is therefore important that church leaders never allow themselves the luxury of believing that because people are active they are stimulated and developing into better persons. They may only feel trapped or guilty about inactivity, or they may like being with a certain set of people in the church. A stimulating and developing church is always evaluating its activity.

Short-Term Objectives and Long-Term Goals

One method of assisting the stimulation process is to use a series of short-range objectives, which can be used to help define and accomplish long-range goals. The term "long-range planning" has fallen into disfavor, and rightly so. Long-range plans are generally proposed in such abstract and general terms as to be out of touch with reality.

A good illustration was the recent opening of the final link of Route I-93 into downtown Boston, Massachusetts. The road, while officially open, will be closed to traffic except at nonrush hours because it is a "road that goes nowhere." The plans, projected some years ago, called for the expressway to proceed across the Charles River and route traffic on up the North Shore. Between the making of the plans and the completion of the road, environmentalists and residents in certain areas through which the expressway was to run protested its completion. They won, and the bridge across the Charles River was not built. Thus, the state discarded plans to complete the North Shore route, and the last link, just opened, brings all traffic into downtown Boston with no exit.

This is not an isolated example of "long-range planning." In fact, many see such planning as the wish of an elite group who have little regard for other people or reality. While the illustration deals with government, the same kind of indictment has plagued the church. Long-range planning in the church is considered an exercise engaged in by persons who talk with other like-minded individuals but know little about the practical world or the day-to-day functioning of the church.

It is true that long-range planning (planning that exceeds the current year) is somewhat risky. It is also true that the plans which finally unfold contain more than a little of the values and assumptions of those who created the plans. Yet there is value in looking ahead and thinking about consequences of various types of activities. If one is really interested in getting things done in the church, it will be necessary to look beyond the present to assess how these activities might affect the church, people and the social situation in three, five and ten years.

The major significance of long-range planning is the looking and dreaming. In the church, dreaming must be concerned with people and their realities. It is dreaming that knows pain and conflict are inevitable, dreaming that seeks to be flexible and ready to change its focus when realities change, dreaming done by many people, not just a few. It is dreaming done in the expectation that the gospel promise will be fulfilled.

In this context, long-range planning becomes a series of short-range objectives and activities, with a duration of one to three months, used to determine, define and accomplish long-range goals. All people have dreams, expectations and desires for the church, but they need a mechanism for helping bring these to fruition. If it can be done a little at a time, this is all that can really be expected. As time goes by, small accomplishments will give people courage and persistence for more daring excursions.

You see, the best encouragement for continuing to strive to meet goals is to accomplish a few lesser goals and achieve some recognition. A person suffering from illness or recovering from an operation has in mind what he hopes to be able to do eventually (a long-range goal). Yet he knows that his doctor will allow him to reach that goal only through short-range accomplishments. He also knows that the uncertainty of healing may cause him to adapt his long-range goals to a more realistic and compromising set of objectives.

"A person walks a hundred miles by taking a step at a time" is a phrase that sums up a philosophy of getting things done within a long-range perspective. Planning is merely looking at oneself, looking at the institution to which one belongs (the church), and at the tools and people with which one has to work in the light of long-term hopes. This is always done in the context of certain social and institutional situations. When these change, it becomes necessary to re-examine each aspect.

A church can evangelize the world only one person at a time. Neighborhoods are changed house by house. Marriages are saved one at a time. Planning is giving things a perspective but working an item at a time. Good planning, the kind that helps the church, insists that jobs be broken into segments so that people can do pieces of jobs rather than be swallowed up in the entire task. It thus becomes possible to redefine direction and redirect energies on relatively short notice.

The church year is a series of segments which, taken as a whole, illustrate the life, death and triumph of Christ. However, the learning and celebration of the year is done daily, weekly and monthly. Could this concept be used in programming as well as in liturgy? Since people's lives are lived in segments—"If I can make it until next month, I will be out of the woods"—let the church take advantage of the psychology of bits and pieces. The church, after all, is not a business organization that must show a profit or loss statement to a board of directors. It is an organization which is attempting to minister to people through people.

Thus, the view one has of the church will affect one's willingness to get involved. The ability of the church to take advantage of people's desire to help get some things done will depend in part upon the willingness of the church to break jobs into segments and pass out the pieces to various persons. This means that the church ought to tap people's interests and skills on *their* time schedule rather than upon the church's.

People's Time Schedules

There are many areas of life in which people can, want to and should be active besides the church. There is nothing wrong with this. Indeed, it is wrong for the church to insist that it be the sole institution to which a person devotes his time and energy. One of the findings of a recent national study was that church people tend to focus their time in the church.[2] This is unfortunate both for them and for the church.

It is unfortunate for them because exposure to only one institution or organization limits the numbers of interests and skills they can use, discover and develop. It is unfortunate for the organization because it robs the organization of a well-rounded person with a multitude of interests. Yet church programming as presently established almost demands complete allegiance and time use. Perhaps because of this, people are either involved in the church fully or not at all.

Given the kind of society in which we live, alternatives to this pattern ought to be considered. The most important need is to recognize that many people can be involved in programs for short periods of time (either as leaders or participants) but cannot make long-term commitments. Some people have schedules that change monthly. It would be best to capitalize upon that kind of schedule rather than penalizing the person for being a policeman, airline employee or service employee. There are also persons whose work load increases or decreases according to time of the year. Again, it is good to work with rather than against such schedules.

If getting things done by and through the church is the name of the game, then the pastor and church leaders might need to reconsider their attitudes toward the use of organization, the manner in which short-range objectives can be used to define and accomplish long-range hopes, and the way in which people are asked to participate in programming. Flexibility must be the key to thinking in organizations. When an organization is faced with situations that allow only segmented participation by a few persons, such participation is much better than none at all. People can make tremendous contributions when given the opportunity to do so within their own time frames, and the church should be able to adjust to that fact.

Practical Theology

Getting things done by revising the thinking and habits of church people represents tremendous change, yet it can be done gradually with a minimum of conflict. In fact, if the approach is one of experimentation with new techniques, very little resistance may be encountered.

On the other hand, with all the emphasis we have so far placed upon gradualism and techniques, there comes the danger that practicalism may become the total theology.

While by no means the intention, this is certainly a danger everyone faces. We tend to worship what we have done. Our accomplishments become an extension of ourselves because they represent an investment of time, energy and talent. We are infatuated with us, and in this sense, pride becomes a corollary of practicalism. Not only do we worship our techniques and methods but we idolize ourselves.

When we have accomplished something, however, we should be recognized for it. In spite of the danger that practicalism will become the altar upon which we worship, practical achievement should not be downgraded. In fact, it must be recognized that theology is a practical set of events, the working out of a basis of meaning within which we can place our everyday experiences. Theology is a set of beliefs or godward looking pegs that can be used to interpret life in all its ebb and flow,[3] and it only becomes meaningful when it finds lodgement in the practical experiences of our daily lives.

One can really theologize about the fellowship of believers only after having an experience that begins to be fellowship. One can read and verbalize nice things about such events, but only the experience itself produces believable theology for most of us. Clergy often speak more meaningfully about such a fellowship than laity because in seminary or other such experiences they have forged a reference point for their discussion. Thus, it is important for theology as a meaning base in one's life to have some concrete reference points of experience upon which to build.

The development of a personal as well as an organizational theology is based upon practical experience. We do something and then we think about what we have done. In the thinking and philosophizing about what we have done, we build our concepts into meaning systems. This means that we have some prior notions about reality and life. Thus, the activity processes of people in a church tend to be a very practical working out of meaning concepts or, in other words, the development of personal theologies. Teaching, leading, attending worship are activities that relate people to the church through experiences they understand and appreciate. They may not know the theological jargon to interpret their activity, but they do know it makes them feel good and it helps others. This is practical theology.

It is practical in the sense that it grows out of our daily lives and experiences. It is theology in the sense that it is given shape and context by the church and its creeds and teachings. Even though ministers may not appreciate the expressions of such theology, the thinking and reacting of people to their experiences is done under the direction and judgment of the gospel and one's understanding of the meaning of Jesus Christ in human life.

One Easter morning an usher and I were standing in the back of the church shortly before the service was to begin. We watched in astonishment as an obviously inebriated local resident, in clothes that had seen many a gutter, came into the church. He walked to the center aisle, genuflected, crossed himself, handed the usher a coin and said, "Good old Greenstone Church" and walked out. We had never seen him before and did not see him again. Yet, he displayed a practical theology. The church was a symbol of what he might hope to become, a symbol of forgiveness, a place of haven. The man had a meaning base, which was pulled together for some of us in this brief encounter.

Our lives are constructed of more or less mundane happenings. In our thought processes we establish patterns of morals and ethics based upon high moments of truth we have experienced with others. For many people, such moments have occurred in the setting of the church, while others are seeking such moments through the church. The activities in which they engage are means to accomplish the hoped-for goal of developing a meaning base. The patterns of morals and ethics lived out through activities of the church help us interpret the meaning of our own actions and lives and the actions and lives of others.

The context of the church, then, is a very important ingredient or means to help people develop a practical theology. It becomes imperative that the church context should contain the stimulation and encouragement of interaction with others in meaningful activities aimed at helping oneself and others. These experiences will include conflict and change. However, the interest, respect and concern in the context of the church will assist the individual to weave new patterns of meanings and behavior out of the more common events of each day.

The church, in the meantime, will be striving to help people work out a basis of meaning in which to place their everyday experiences. This will be done, as expressed by one layman, by "getting the church going . . . (developing) a sense of purpose . . . (and getting) people interested and involved." A practical theology would thereby be developing for the organization while new learnings and attitudes of individuals about themselves and others were being incorporated into a broadened meaning system. Doing theology is much more effective than talking about a theology. When it is done, it is a part of us. When we talk about it, it is an abstract idea presented to us by others. Christ lived a theology. Perhaps that is the best guide we can find to developing a practical theology.

Questions for Discussion

1. How does self-interest express itself in your involvement in the church? in your theology?
2. Do you feel that your activity in the church is beneficial to others? Why?
3. How can the church use its desire for activity to stimulate people? Does the church need to change the focus and shape of those activities? In what ways?
4. Have you or your church taken the time to dream about what it could be? Have you tried to think through those dreams to develop practical plans for making the dreams reality?

8 change and organizations

Changes have hit organizations especially hard during the past two decades. Max Weber described the typical bureaucratic organization as a hierarchy built upon disciplined and ordered small groups,[1] then gathered into large complexes of bosses and bossed. His framework or model was the German army of the early 1900's.

In a small book published in 1971,[2] George Berkley writes about "The Crumbling Pyramid," "The End of Organization Man," "The Era of the Client" and "Shelter without Walls." His thesis is that the structure described so well by Weber and the management experts after him is no longer viable. People are not willing to be caught up in a big machine in which they are but a small part. They are not willing to provide money and status to persons who produce little of benefit but who "keep the machinery running."

No one who has observed the church for a period of time would deny that change is stirring it up. The people in the pews are being discovered as not passive but quite insistent that their point of view be considered seriously. It was no surprise that a majority of the church people interviewed in a recent international study indicated that they wanted more say in how and which programs were developed in their churches.[3] They supported the necessity of the denomination, but were insisting that the denomination stop being an impersonal address and become an instrument to help with their problems. In fact, they were ready to specify how that help should be given: counsel and guidance in their churches.

The need for change in the church has been around for awhile but it is just now taking revolutionary form. The church has attempted to model its organization on a business, emphasizing efficiency and rational behavior. This emphasis, while needed for bookkeeping, program design and implementation, has a stifling effect when carried over beyond its time. Its time is past not only in business but in the church.

There are good reasons for this rebellion against bureaucracy. In the first place, there has been a tremendous increase in the sophistication of people in the pews, and one aspect of sophistication is that it reduces the awe of power. Many church persons can do better program planning and implementation than those who are in places of authority in the churches. This is not to shortchange the capabilities of church program developers. It is to indicate that they are not dealing with an unenlightened or incapable laity at the local level.

Secondly, people in the pew are aware of their own capacities. In their areas of expertise, they can see little reason to depend upon others for complete program development. This is a part of the demand that the organization make room for local and regional initiative in program development.

Thirdly, the organization, as it was developed through the 1950's at least, did not really have the person in mind. True, it did give lip service to the person but planning and programs were constructed in paternalistic fashion, like a father telling his children they could think or act on their own.

The rebellion of the people in the pews has resulted in a series of denominational restructures. These have not been piddling changes of positions on organization charts. They have been fundamental changes in the philosophy of what an organization should and can do for and with people. New structural forms, new representation patterns including women, youth, minorities and new styles of functioning including attempts at collegial staffs and matrix functioning have emerged. Not a great deal of experience has been accumulated in any of these new styles, but they are a part of the structures being implemented by several denominations in the early 1970's.

The restructure pattern has also made the various levels of the organization much more amenable to local needs and interests. In the local church this has found a counterpart in an effort to be more understanding of diversity of opinion. The bare fact is that the organizations are being bent by the people who are supposed to be served by them into a vehicle that can be meaningful to them.

There is relatively little anti-institutionalism as such. People know that organizations are necessary and important to achieve goals in a complex society. There is a strong current of "if that organization doesn't serve us, we will change it until it does." This attitude is not lost upon leaders and shapers of organizations. They are having a bit of a time breaking out of bureaucratic patterns of working and thinking, but they know that unless they do someone is waiting to assume their task and reshape it to current demands.

These changes are more than a little frightening to many people. Order and stability are important in organizations and societies. People need a base that can be used to reflect their own identity and purpose in life, and organizations have served these functions for many. When order and stabiltiy are threatened, people become anxious about themselves. They are the organization and to change it is to change them. Most have little to gain in such changes.

Yet change is a tidal wave of human need pushing and hauling organizations like boats caught in the open sea. The captain is helpful as a symbol but is useless as a leader for he, too, is caught in the midst of a crisis and is seeking guidance. Destruction will overtake many persons caught in this era who are depending upon stability and order. On the other hand, there is always the opportunity to move somewhat gracefully with change in an organization and to make it work for both the people and the organization. This can be done most easily by examining a few facts about the way organizations change. As these are examined it can become apparent how we who are caught in the midst of the changes can adjust and help the church organization to adjust, so that its movement toward the people will not be overwhelming and defeat the very purpose of the change.

Institutions Are Always Changing

The first fact is apparent—perhaps. Institutions are never stable. We think they are stable because we only live on their outskirts and have little to do with the dynamics that keep them alive, or because we focus upon the written rules and observe the constant symbols of the organization. (Even the symbols are changing now, however. One gas company kept its tiger while it changed its name so that people would still recognize the company.) If one could move into the depths of an organization, regardless of whether that organization were a PTA or a local church or a political party, one would discover that the inside was a changing dynamo of persons and ideas.

A person who attends worship regularly in a local church but has little other participation in that church may think the church is structured and ordered and certainly could not classify as changing. If that person had the opportunity to become a part of the administrative and planning committees of the church, he or she would be enlightened and sometimes disheartened by the degree of change taking place. Programs are adopted, tried and dropped. Ideas are proposed, opposed and discussed beyond recognition. Enthusiasm is generated and just as quickly dies away into inaction. Yet the church keeps going and doing. In this one can take heart.

Thus, there are at least three components to the changing of institutions. First, people flow in and out of leadership positions and in so doing create flows, patterns and opportunities for the organization. Second, ideas are always being introduced and tested. As this occurs, especially when new persons are introduced into membership and leadership, the organization receives a series of jolts similar to electric shock treatments. Third, there is a continual gap between the ideal and the actual in an organization. In fact, organizations operate as a compromise with great allegiance to the possible rather than the ideal. These three factors are never really separable in practice, but for our purpose it is helpful to discuss each in order.

It takes but little imagination and experience to verify that people moving through an organization, either in its membership or its leadership, create new patterns of functioning and opportunity. Perhaps the most critical of the two flows is that of leadership. Since most voluntary organizations have rules that limit the length of time people can hold office, it is a way of life to be always in the process of training new leaders. They need to be taught the ways of thinking and acting in their positions so that the organization can continue to perform its stated activities and fulfill its purpose.

It is evident to any who have had to train leaders that no two persons are alike. Some catch on quickly and adjust their patterns of thinking and acting quite well, while others persist in their old habits and do not want to make adjustments. In both cases, however, the persons interpret the positions on the basis of their own past experiences and histories. Even words take on different meaning for different people. A simple word like retreat may be quite appealing to some persons whose experiences have been helpful, and quite the opposite for a person whose experiences have been less than positive. Experience determines the manner of interpretation.

It is because of this variable in new leaders that organizations tend to like to retain the old leaders. They are predictable, if not really creative and in tune with present needs. This dependability of leadership is one of the points at which change becomes personal and frightening. A pastor often finds it more comfortable to stay in a parish than to move to another which would allow him and that parish to change habits and thought patterns. Nominating committees in local churches like to use the same people over and over, rotating them among jobs, because they know how these persons will function.

One cannot really blame organizational leaders for attempting to surround themselves with persons with whom they feel most comfortable. However, there is a limit, and events in the world and the church indicate that the limit has been reached. The flow through of persons can no longer be in a circle; it must actually be *through* leadership positions. Others can and should be involved. As frightening as this may seem, unless organizations are willing to make sure that new leaders are introduced, the organizations are going to feel the pangs of death or the throes of revolution. Neither is pleasant, but both are over in relatively short periods of time.

New persons usually do things differently. Most of us tend to think in rather standard terms. We try to improve what we are already doing but are very resistant to new activities. We do attempt "innovations" occasionally, but these generally have been tried elsewhere and results are rather predictable. This is not to downgrade modifications as change makers. It is to indicate that such changes are continuous but generally not startling.

Change becomes startling with new ideas. This is one of the most amazing things about current organizational changes. Not only activities, but the entire philosophy of what organizations are or should be, are being changed. A totally new set of ideas is being generated and implemented into structures.

It is the intangibleness of these concepts that strikes terror to our bones. You see, we are creatures of habit. We need to function on habit most of the time because of the multiplicity of decisions we need to make. We need to react automatically to danger, whether physical or emotional; we need to retain our perspective on ourselves even when we change groups and situations. We do these things without thinking, for they are ingrained in our psyches.

In this same way, we have internalized our concepts of what certain types of organizations are and should be. We do not think it strange that worship, education and fellowship are integral to the church—but we would think it strange should a business organization feel that its activities should include worship and Christian education. We have developed stereotypes inside ourselves, which have tended to protect both ourselves and the institutions to which we belong. Little wonder, then, that when these habits of thoughts are called into question, we react with negativism, if not anxiety.

It is therefore the *idea* that is potentially the most threatening of all change agents. Yet man lives in a world of ideas and hopes—exciting, challenging and frightening. Movies are acted out ideas in the same way that literature and stories are written out ideas. Churches are ideas that have been codified into beliefs and creeds. Ideas are of the nature of humanity.

Perhaps for this very reason, ideas are never really stable or ordered. They are like lightening bolts that flash out of clear skies. They catch the interest of others and cannot be let go. They are discussed and thought about and gotten hold of. They are worried over and adjusted to new situations and experiences. Just about the time they get comfortable, another idea or offshoot of the first comes into focus and another process of testing, thinking and trying occurs.

Have you ever heard an idea expressed in a church meeting to which the only sensible reaction was that the person was out of her or his element? Just think about some of the ideas that have come through the church. Love one another, give to those who despise you, give your cloak also, go into all the world to preach the gospel . . . Strange, fascinating and unworkable. Just as unworkable and as far out as rockets and moon landings, energy from a neutron, a black woman refusing to take a back seat in the bus. Preposterous are some of the ideas people have—and express through the church. It is no wonder the organization has to change to accommodate some of them.

Ideas change people slowly. Yet there are some ideas which come with the crushing force of a bulldozer. They come in time and meet a particular and peculiar need of the people to whom they are presented. They are right ideas. Not one of us would be wise enough to sort out those ideas from all the rest that we hear and read about. It is good that the church exists to provide a context for new ideas. If these make us change a bit either in our thinking or acting, who is the better for it?

One of the observable and very much documented facts about the church is that there is a difference between what it preaches and what it does. The same is true of us. We know what we should do but there is a credibility or at least a performance gap. Our aim in life is to narrow that gap to workable proportions. In the process of narrowing the gap, change takes place.

It may take place as people attempt to rethink the purpose of an organization or try to practice some of the rules of the organization. One of the most interesting events in a strike of supervisors on the New York subway system in the early 1970's was that they staged a "slowdown" by observing all the rules in their manuals—and thereby speeded up the trains! If the supervisors had followed the rules all the time, the subway would have been improved considerably.

In every institution there is such a distance between hopes and performance. The church, since it deals with meanings and values, is often more aware of the gap than other institutions. Perhaps because of this awareness, church people are often unwilling or at least hesitant to proclaim the meaning of the Christian imperative by condemning unethical acts and various forms of non-Christian behavior.

When the gap becomes noticeable, there arise prophets or at least persons who feel it their duty to set the church back on its original course. Their criticism is necessary although often irritating and grating. No one really likes to hear that their task is being done poorly, even if that task is merely sitting through a worship service. We like to be made to feel comfortable, whether or not we are actually fulfilling the purposes of our organization. If we are doing something that remotely fits in with the purposes, and if we feel it is worthwhile, we are generally content to let things proceed.

Fortunately, there are those who feel an obligation to become the stimulators for perfection. They recognize, as do we, that all institutions function on compromises rather than ideals, but their aim is to move the organization closer to the ideal. The Old Testament is replete with stories of persons who have called religious leaders to task for not fulfilling their duties. The church has had its share of divisions caused by the conviction that the church had strayed from its calling.

Being called to account for the difference between profession and action is quite a stimulus to change. It is very effective when those around us also realize that change is necessary and a commitment is made by several persons to accomplish certain changes. When these changes are implemented (such as attending worship regularly), certain things begin to happen in the institution. Efforts are made by leaders to recruit new leaders, new or differing emphases are given to activities and a climate of renewed interest begins to be kindled.

It would be simplistic to assume that changes always happen. But the power of a changed person is very great, and when commitment becomes expressed in visible terms, other persons in an organization begin to note the change and there is a chain effect.

In all of this positivism it should be emphasized that even with change in an organization, the organization will still function more along the lines of what is probable than what is possible. There is little chance that even with great changes in churches or people an organization will be other than a vehicle that assists people in being somewhat better able to deal with reality. In other words, the church will not reach its ideals. It will continue to function where its members need it. It will continue to be a compromise between God and people.

We can rejoice in hope, however. We can and must continue to push the organization toward its ideals, with each generation reinterpreting those ideals through its realities.

Change Is Not Disruptive

It becomes clear, then, that there are tremendous forces pushing and pulling institutions and causing them to change. Most of the instigators of change are people who come and go, ideas that are expressed and sometimes find their day, and a pressure to reach for the ideals and not be content with the standard way of doing things. Even with these pressures for change, one should not assume that change is always disruptive. When change is used well, it is a creative event or series of events in the lives of people and churches. Only when change is resisted and thwarted does it become filled with danger and disaster.

Yet, change must sometimes be resisted or else the human becomes only an organism pushed by seemingly uncontrollable force. This is most important when those forces pushing changes are affecting the human organism.

On the other hand, if organizations do not change, there will continue to be institutions that are totally irrelevant to people. For instance, the Flat Earth Society persists even with pictures from space to show clearly that the earth is not flat. People and resources are locked into a society without any practical benefit except to a few leaders.

Some have said that change in organizations must move slowly to preserve the meaning, status and stability of those most affected by it. This has been the admonition of many local church leaders. Acting under the conflicting pressures of pull and tug in both directions, toward and against change, such leaders have neutralized the pull by insisting upon listening to the tug of those against change. Their argument is that change is too disruptive. Yet these same people proceed to fly on airplanes, drive new automobiles, use new gadgets in their home and at work. There is a basic inconsistency, at least on the surface.

Not necessarily true. Change is really an attitude toward trying the new or innovating practices and procedures. The use of new gadgets and tools has little to do with change, at least in the minds of a great many people. Change really takes place when people's relationships are stirred. The use of a computer is viewed as good when it relieves the drudgery of a good number of clerks—but not when it is impossible to get "personalized service" if things go awry with a billing.

It is this separation between things and people which allows some people to accept certain types of innovations but strongly resist changes that affect their relations with others. Since the church is concerned primarily with people, events and relations, there is good reason why it often feels the protective hand of resistance to change more than other types of organizations. People have come to expect certain types of people processes to occur at the church, and to disturb these processes is to unbalance the stability of meaning systems. It is not that people resist change per se but that it is not included in their understanding of human relationships.

The point is, however, that because people change in their understanding of life, their experience and needs, the relationships that make up institutions and organizations must also change. One of the prime tasks of the church may be to help people develop an appreciation and an impetus for change in their relationships within the church. This task is essential, and it is also difficult. It involves building a new value system, which includes attitudes and beliefs accepting of change and yet critical enough that change is not accepted just to be different.

Such a process is difficult in individuals, and even more so in organizations. The nature of a voluntary organization could assist in keeping the spirit of change alive and well, however. Because institutions are always changing, as we have seen, the potential for creative change has been established. Oh! if it were only that simple! In many ways it is simple, but it does take effort and time. The key is to create a climate that allows people to develop a perspective that includes change. Evaluation and review of the purpose and functioning of an organization are essential ingredients in building a climate of change.

Only when there is an exchange of ideas about purpose and operations by persons committed to the organization is there hope for establishing an attitude of change. Once the attitude is established, changes can be implemented.

It is true, then, that human relationships can be developed to become adaptable to changing situations. This happens in marriages that last long periods of time. It occurs in relations between parents and children over decades. There is a recognition that what is now will not be next year or several years from now. The child of today is a mature individual in a decade or two. The same is true of organizations. The web of friendships and leaderships needs to be built in such a way that they are both strong and flexible.

An organization that has as one of its continuing goals the developing and strengthening of human relationships must have several mechanisms for helping people meet change.

The organization will provide many opportunities for informal contacts between leaders and members. In such meetings the primary objective is to let each group see the issues facing them from another person's perspective. The issues can be as large as building a building or as small as explaining the policy for building use. Any issue, given the opportunity for people to take sides and become identified with a particular position, is explosive. When there is a mechanism established by the organization to help people understand each other before and during issue discussion, the process of making change in a supportive manner has begun.

One cannot overstress the importance of informal processes for helping people meet new ideas, persons and issues. It is difficult at best to continually compromise; it is extremely unsettling to have to compromise during a battle that could have occurred in a different setting where reason could have taken precedence over emotion. The organization that attempts to help people develop lasting relationships will provide the arena for such discussions.

Change—the Past, Present and Future

Change is more than wrenching old ways of behaving out of the present. In fact, change in organizations is very aware of both the past and the future in relation to the present. Organizations as well as people have heritages and histories. In fact, many organizations began as the dream of a small group of people who were convinced that something new was needed in their day. They started an adventure which became an institution.

When one begins to think about change in organizations, it is well to look back through the records to discover who had made similar proposals, and when. Recently a sociologist had completed a historical review of an organization which he felt needed to be redirected. In the review he discovered that nearly twenty years earlier proposals similar to his had been suggested by the very leaders he had thought were backward and totally resistant to change. He was surprised at the foresight of past generations.

An old history professor frequently told a class, "There is nothing new under the sun." While this is true in a strict sense, people have been able to combine old elements to make startling changes in environments, technologies and organizations. The point is not lost in spite of these new combinations. Humankind has been around for quite awhile and the problems of organizations today have had antecedents. The solutions to these problems also have parallels in previous times.

It is possible to learn from history, particularly the history of the organization one wishes to change. This learning can provide the precedent for introducing changes that may, in effect, return the organization to its original purpose. More likely, the learning can provide an understanding of the intent of the organization and a feel for its spirit, both of which are needed if and when change is suggested.

The past is the record of an organization's struggle for its identity and purpose. This record should be selectively used to help the organization adapt to the present even while it is projecting a realistic future. In other words, long-term expectations for an organization should find some rootage in its heritage, but that heritage should not become a millstone. Today is different in context and content from yesterday. Tomorrow will be different also. The trick is to find the combination of long-term hopes, practical orientations and appreciation and understanding of the past to help us in the process of changing institutions.

When we take the time to look both ways from the present, we have a much better opportunity to introduce change that is not too threatening or disruptive. Institutions, especially churches, are composed of persons from several generations, and all need to receive respect and recognition for their contribution. This means that even in radical change proposals, homage must be given to those who were pioneers of an earlier day.

Change does not always have to be disruptive. Our approach to change and our appreciation of people, past, present and future, will make it less so. We still need a great deal of humility for our little knowledge and desires for a new day. Others have stood and will stand where we are now. As persons in a stream of history, how can we best develop the organizations to which we belong so that the heritage of today can be bent and reused tomorrow? Change is the inevitable human experience, especially in organizations.

Questions for Discussion

1. What is the real cause of reorganization in the church?
2. How important to you and to members of your church is order and stability of the church?
3. How do you and your church deal with the different viewpoints of leaders who are new?
4. How do you treat new ideas in your church? What long-term effect do they generally have?
5. How can you ensure that change in your church will not be disruptive?

9 a new mystery

The Scopes "monkey" trial in 1925 was a dispute over how the idea of creation should be taught. The State of Tennessee wanted schools to teach only the biblical interpretation of God taking seven days to create the earth and all living things. J. T. Scopes wanted to teach the evolutionary theory of human development from lower forms of life. At issue was the *myth* base of society. J. T. Scopes was trying to establish a new myth based upon facts as defined by the scientific community. Indeed, this new myth was a scientific as opposed to a biblical interpretation of creation.

In 1973, the same state of Tennessee passed a law requiring that any textbook discussing creation give equal time to the biblical story and to the evolutionary theory. The significance of the 1973 law is not so much that Tennessee still clings to its 1925 position but that it recognizes the need for multiple myths.

The myths that have guided people through centuries have been wrapped in religious images. Beliefs and rituals have been used to explain the unknowable. God has been a spirit or spirits that had a hand in creating, sustaining and tormenting people. God has been given the attributes of anger, happiness and pleasure. No civilization of record has not used some religion in explaining the unexplainable events that shape human experience.

The underlying reason for such explanations is that people must try to pinpoint the causes for "natural" events such as floods, volcanos and storms. When the causes are not readily evident, and even the scientific explanations do not remove the dread and fear of natural disaster, the human mind draws upon its own resources to create reasons.

This is not capriciously done. People through history have built their reasoned myths upon the most feasible logic. It did not seem illogical (and still does not to many people) to explain good seasons and bad ones by saying that these depended upon the anger or the pleasure of the gods. Neither does it seem unreasonable to ascribe healing and death to the wishes of unknown forces controlled by a god or gods.

The development of myths is a recognition that there is a

point beyond which human knowledge cannot go. Even when people have turned on all the lights of their thought and experience, there still remains an impenetrable darkness. This unknown surrounds and resides in people. It is an intriguing and a frightening part of a person's being, a magnet that draws people into a search for the unknowable. It is the reason that people are "incurably religious." [1]

The changing nature of our world and the increased importance attached to science has, during the past century or two, allowed the development of a myth built upon science. This myth has the same characteristics of the religious myth, that is, of trying to explain the unknowable, but there are some very important differences in terminology.

These variations of terms highlight the key difference between religious and scientific-based myths. While both must rely upon a "leap of faith" to link human experiences with the unknown, the difference is the scientific method.

The scientific method is a process of asking the "why" question until answers are found or explanations constructed. As much verifiable data as is available is examined for possible proof or causes of events. Postulates of how these explain the unknown are then developed. The advocates of this method look down upon the nonrational basis of other methods. They are especially hard on the religious way of explaining things.

Yet the narrowness of science has been attacked recently by various parts of the society. The mood of these attacks is that science has pushed too far and there must be more concern for the humanization of technology. The scientific method accomplishes a great deal, but *truth* is not necessarily found by this method. Information is discovered, but truth is a combination of information and human interpretative wisdom.

The expressed need for having more than science and its method as a basis for human understanding is indicative of the search for a new myth. Science has produced new bombers, new bombs and new gadgets for use in space but it has produced precious little in the way of helping humans to protect their environment, get along with each other or find an ultimate purpose in life. Indeed these are not discoverable through the use of the scientific method, as the people who are following the occult, eastern religions and charismatic movements testify. The scientific method can only be used in the search for information.

It is essential to develop myths because people need to be committed to something beyond themselves. They must have a purpose that somehow deals with the unknowable, the real world of experience and the hoped for world of dreams.

People do not live by bread alone. They live because of a tenaciousness of being that seems to be inborn. This desire can be beaten through time and corrupted by people's experiences of meaninglessness, but it does spring up over and over again. It is perhaps the most powerful force in humans.

Jesus Christ is the Christian's prime example of this combination of higher purpose and desire to live. The decision to take the high road was not easy to come by. Jesus took time alone in a garden to contemplate the decision. In the end, the cry of "Why hast thou forsaken me?" (Matt. 27:46) showed even Jesus' strong desire to find answers to the unknowable ways of God.

The need for commitment is also based upon people's desire to have their place in the universe of things identified. Commitment to something and/or someone gives them a sense of stability and of purpose. There is an old game of "Who am I?" that might personify the eternal question of people.

Some might answer this question by saying, "I'm a doctor," or "I'm a Communist" or "I'm a Connecticut Yankee." Each of these identities involves a history as well as a specific person. The players make the identification of who the persons are by specifying the attachments they have to others, to organizations and to ideologies. These attachments provide a stabliity to the game because the players know that there are ingredients to a life which tend not to change. These ingredients usually hinge upon what the person has committed oneself to and how that commitment has been acted out in experience.

A recent book on extrasensory perception in Russia told that each person has an envelope of air and charged particles surrounding her or him. This envelope is an invisible extension of oneself. It becomes a protector because any disturbance of that envelope generates change of some sort within or upon the person.

In the same way, people build social and ideological or belief boxes around themselves. That's the reason change in status, identifying or belief systems is so threatening. When one attacks what seems like an institutional practice, one needs to understand that people in the institution have used that practice as a means of building their own personal stability and identity. That practice is one of the planks of their identity. The salute of an officer by a nonofficer may seem ridiculous to those who oppose a military way of life, but the identities of both parties are built upon the separation of responsibilities and privileges, of which the salute is but a symbol.

Changes that affect our personal, social or belief boxes

become threats to our identity and purpose. These changes are resisted as a reflex action. Many people who advocate change are quite aware of this. Others are not and so, in their enthusiasm to correct seemingly outdated and unnecessary status practices, unknowingly attack people and their sense of worth and integrity. Science as a community has done this to religious believers, to the point where admitting a belief has been a source of embarrassment. Science won for a while in its mythology but it is now losing the war for people's ultimate allegiance.

The importance of the idea of people living in boxes leads to three observations about commitment and living. These observations are given so that we in the Christian community can better deal with change while sustaining people's sense of individual worth and personal integrity.

In the first place, people's lives are generally lived in pieces or segments, and thus their commitments are also made in pieces and segments. Not many people take the time or have an interest in looking at themselves and their lives as totalities. Part of the reason is that there is no real perspective point from which one can view a life. Most of us recognize that the best perspective is gained by those who survive. Since so few of us survive our own life, it is a bit impractical to suggest that we take advantage of that particular perspective.

Most of us also resist planning our lives. We make decisions on an impulse or somewhat rational basis and do not really plan what we would eventually want to be. Many of us are thankful that this has been the case. When we read of someone who carefully worked out a plan for life and then followed it, we become a little envious and even feel guilty for a time. However, we soon feel a bit grateful that our experience has been a collage rather than a linear experiment in living.

At best, life is a series of seemingly unrelated experiences. The time at work, the time at home, the time at play all seem somehow disjointed except that *we* were at all of them. When we think about putting all these experiences together, it becomes a chore and the spontaneity of the experiences is lost.

This points to a second dilemma regarding commitment. There is a wholeness to life but a major problem we have is to discover how all the pieces or segments fit together to make the whole. A family money management service has a series of books and aids designed to help people look at themselves financially in terms of wholeness. One magazine has a regular feature in which a family meets with consultants to help the family examine its finances in the whole.

One need not read more than a few of these features to understand that there is a common tendency for people *not* to look at themselves wholly. It is also clear that financial commitments are not made in terms of money so much as other factors, most of which deal with identity and past experience.

It is not always appropriate to suggest that people ought to get a holistic view of themselves and their commitments. It does help to do exactly that once in awhile and, in fact, regularly. This is not to develop a rigid plan of attack for life but to see where one's commitments might eventually lead.

Dramatic examples of people who did take the time to assess their commitments were often noted in the now defunct *Life* magazine. There were stories about executives who left the market place for a more down-to-earth life in small town America, whether on the plains or on its rocky coasts. These people did not lose their skills but expanded their life to include other skills. More importantly, they began to live their commitments in a whole package rather than in the hectic segmentalized world that can characterize metropolitan executives.

The hippies have perhaps been the stimulus that has forced our society to reexamine its commitments and wholeness. Their open rejection of convention and standards forced a confrontation at first, but has allowed most of us a sense of freedom to consider our own reasons for acting and thinking in certain ways.

What the hippies have done for society at large, the youth and charismatic movements have done for the church. A rethinking of the purpose of the church has been heavily influenced by the presence if not the actions of these persons. The church has been enamored of science and its message for several decades now. It has been unpopular to be religious in church except in rather conventional and stylized ways. The charismatic movement emphasizes the need for emotion, nonconvention and freedom for the Spirit to move. There are some within the church who feel that this revitalized openness is really the hope of the future.

This, then, points to the third facet of commitments. Seeing the whole helps one to discover what the commitments are in one's life. When the whole is seen there can be new excitment so that even the everyday humdrum things take on new meaning. An ad on TV regarding glaucoma talks about the vividness of seeing. While physical sight is not exactly what is meant here, it does lend itself to an illustration. Seeing or gaining insight is like a person who suddenly gains vision. The beauty of the world is breath-catching and even the dull spots have taken on a luster not known before.

Being "born again" is the term used to designate a new vision of reality caused by a change in life's purpose through the intervention of the Holy Spirit. In this age of pluralism and change, these might not be the appropriate words but the experience they convey is the same. It is having a single focused life rather than a series of scattered and separate focuses for activities. At the center, for a Christian, is or should be the life and teachings of Jesus Christ.

The need is ever present to develop new understandings of the meaning of life. Whether we ascribe to a fundamentally religious or a primarily scientific myth regarding the ultimate purpose of life, we need each other in our common search. Indeed, we need to join forces in committing ourselves to the task of discovering the unknown. Truth is in such scarce supply that no one of us or our methods is able to find enough to last for long periods of time.

A new set of myths, which incorporate the learnings of the human search for reality and ultimacy and a more rigorous testing of hypotheses about reality, need to be worked at. Since this is the NOW generation, it appears that we are assigned that opportunity.

Enviable that task is, too. Interchange of experience and purpose can enlighten and inform. It can motivate and inspire. It can develop a meaning that would never be possible if we stayed behind the shutters of our little boxes.

Change is here and we must deal with it. Change can provide us a freedom to ask questions we would never have dared to ask a few years ago. As we question, it is necessary to look at life and its purpose in the wholeness of our own experiences and dreams. We must also commit ourselves to a purpose that goes far beyond what we can ever achieve on our own. In the process, we shall discover and incorporate a new mystery, a mystery of being that will be a combination of the "old, old story" and the age of technology and computers.

Questions for Discussion

1. What are the basic myths upon which your life is founded?
2. How do you explain the unknowable? Do you think others should explain it in the same manner? Can you really think about your manner of faith in terms of myth?
3. How often do you try to look at your life holistically? What do you see?
4. How often does your church look at its life holistically? What does it see?
5. What are your really important commitments in life? Are they in keeping with the demands of Jesus Christ upon us as disciples?

notes

Chapter 2
1. C. West Churchman, *The Systems Approach*. New York: Dell Publishing Company, 1968.

Chapter 3
1. M. Dean Kelley, *Why Conservative Churches Are Growing*. New York: Harper and Row, 1972.
2. Douglas W. Johnson and George W. Cornell, *Punctured Preconceptions*. New York: Friendship Press, 1972.
3. William Bruce Cameron, *Modern Social Movements*. New York: Random House, 1966.

Chapter 4
1. A. Campbell and E. E. Converse (eds.). New York: 1972.

Chapter 6
1. Thomas A. Harris, *I'm O.K.—You're O.K.* New York: Harper and Row, 1969.

Chapter 7
1. Johnson and Cornell, *op. cit.*
2. *Ibid.*
3. Earl D. C. Brewer, "Religion in Elementary Forms of Everyday Life," unpublished paper. United Methodist Task Force on Religious Indicators, Dayton, Ohio, 1972.

Chapter 8
1. Max Weber, "The Types of Authority," in Talcott Parsons, et al. (eds.), *Theories of Societies*. Glencoe, Ill.: The Free Press, 1961, Vol. 1, pp. 626-632.
2. George E. Berkley, *The Administrative Revolution*. Englewood Cliffs, N.J.: Prentice-Hall, Inc., 1971.
3. Johnson and Cornell, *op. cit.*

Chapter 9
1. Andrew M. Greeley, *The Unsecular Man*. New York: Schocken Books, 1972.